# TRY AND MAKE ME!

## POWER STRUGGLES:

*A Book of Strategies for Adults Who Live and Work with Angry Kids*

By
Penny Cuninggim
EDD, MSW

*In this book, Dr. Cuninggim captures the heart and soul of the at-risk children with whom so many of us struggle each day. Her love, strength, firmness and wisdom make this book a must read for anyone engaged in the daily battle to harness the myriad of outrageous behaviors these kids throw at us. Try and Make Me is the culmination of years of work and provides a sophisticated set of strategies that help each of us deepen our relationships with both our own children and the children in our care. Brava!*

Steven Bengis, ED.D., L.C.S.W.
Executive Director, New England Adolescent
Research Institute, Inc.

*Power struggles are at the heart of so many disputes between children and adults, institutions, and even nations. While there are political and philosophical works on this subject, prior to Cuninggim's book, a practical, down-to-earth, no-nonsense resource did not exist. This is a must read for every teacher or parent interacting with young people. As an educator, I believe this book should be required reading for teachers entering the educational field and for every parent before they except the responsibility of children.*

Dr. Farideh Seihoun
Assistant to the Superintendent,
Chicopee Public Schools, Chicopee, MA

# *Try and Make Me!*

*Power Struggles: A Book of Strategies for Adults
Who Live and Work With Angry Kids*
Copyright©2004 Penny Cuninggim

*Published by*
## NEARI Press
70 North Summer Street
Holyoke, MA 01040
413.540.0712

*Distributed by*
## Whitman Distribution
10 Water Street • PO Box 1220
Lebanon, New Hampshire 03766
603.448.0037 • 800.353.3730
ISBN# 1-929657- 23-4
Price US $15.00

# Dedication

This book is dedicated to all the kids with whom I have been in power struggles in my life. These kids include my own two children, Amanda and Corey, as well as hundreds of school, after-school, therapy and residential youth with whom I have worked over the years. You have taught me all I know about what not to do.

This book is also dedicated to the 300+ professionals with whom I have teamed over the past twenty-five years. With little support and no paradigms, we began working with extremely volatile youth during early "deinstitutionaliza-tion". Over the years, we created a unique intervention model out of our muscle, mental grit and tears. Today, we continue to experiment, study new research, refine our approaches, and systematically share our ideas with others. You, my colleagues, have operated with a raw courage, a healthy dismissal of all the naysayers, and a steadfast belief that we could work successfully with children whom others said could not be treated in community-based settings. As my life-long pals in the trenches, my images of your creative and caring interventions give me strength to keep working with angry kids, when I think I have nothing left to give.

## *My Thanks To...*

Steven Bengis, my husband and colleague, for his ever present support, his sharp mind, and his careful critiques.

Whitty Cuninggim, my mom, for both her sustained belief that I have something useful to say, and her precise edits from first page to last.

Dr. Vicki Levi, friend, colleague and mentor, for giving me the idea and then pushing me to write this one first.

Sue Everett, my friend and colleague of twenty-five years, who, as we ran, then walked, now stroll on our weekly treks through the New England countryside, gabs with me about all the crazy interventions we have done together over the years.

Brett Averitt, Rita Bleiman, Carol Edelstein, Cynthia Kennison, Lida Lewis, Tanyss Martula, Nanny Prior, and Renee Schultz, members of my writers group, who provided me with invaluable feedback all along the way. Thanks to Carol for the (perfect) title too.

Diane Langelier, Steve Leiblum, Mike McCormic, Izzy Ortiz, Wednesday Sorokin, and Dan Williamson, all colleagues in the work, who reviewed the manuscript and provided me with both invaluable insights and detailed edits.

Rob Longo, my NEARI Press editor, who waited so patiently, and then as the book emerged, gave me critically important suggestions and served as a steady, nurturing "container" of support.

# Contents

# *Why and For Whom Is This Book Written?*

I believe power struggles are at the heart of most negative inter-actions we have with combative children. Yet, this topic has not been part of any course or workshop I have ever taken, nor have I found much of depth written on power strug-gles in professional or parenting books and magazines. Authors tend to say the same (brief) thing: When it comes to power struggles with kids, don't get into them in the first place.

These authors' emphases tend to be on larger realms, such as violence prevention and "aggression replacement" training, responding to teenage moodiness and rebelliousness, dealing with different kinds of negative temperaments and attitudes, responding proactively to varying levels of physical aggression, de-escalating acting out behaviors, and developing conflict resolution strategies. Although such manuals and books might devote a few pages to power struggles, this topic is not the main focus.

This book is written solely about power struggles and for adults who, on a regular basis, interact with angry, combative children and youth. Two adult groups, teachers and parents, are clearly ones who first come to mind. By virtue of their roles, as well as their daily contact with kids, these two adult groups, in home or classroom, must establish social rules of order. Their similar role mandates involve pushing children to grow, develop and learn important lessons. In turn, their child charges naturally push back. As these adults set essential routines, expectations, and rules, they serve as weathervanes, attracting resistance and providing space for boundary testing. Such struggling is a uni-versal theme, a necessary passage, as children move from one stage of development to the next.

Other adults relating to such children who could also benefit from this book include, educators, child care workers, social workers, foster parents, therapists, and lay people who may not have professional training or a primary care-taking role with combative children, but who nevertheless occasionally interact with angry kids.

Each of you responds to power struggles every time you relate to unhappy children who want to fight with you. I suppose, in the end, no matter one's adult role, when relating to a combative kid, just one exchange gone awry qualifies you as someone who could benefit from this book.

## Chapter One

# *Gotcha!*

Hello and welcome to the world of Power Struggles.

Before reading any further in this book, be sure to read through this entire page. After you have read this page, turn to the next page and ask a friend/colleague to help you with this exercise.

On the next page, there is a list of phrases. Tell your friend or colleague you are going to close your eyes while that person slowly reads each phrase out loud to you. Be prepared for some unsavory words. As each phrase is spoken aloud to you, say the first thing that comes to your mind. Repeat this process back and forth for each phrase on the page. Be as spontaneous as you can. Do not second-guess your thoughts. Just see what comes out of your mouth.

When the person reading to you gets to the bottom of the page, have him/her stop and ask you to open your eyes. Then turn to the page that follows the list of phrases.

YOU CAN'T MAKE ME.

LEAVE ME ALONE.

YOU CAN'T TELL ME WHAT TO DO.

YOU'RE NOT THE BOSS OF ME.

YOU DON'T KNOW WHAT I FEEL.

NO ONE IS GONNA LISTEN TO YOU ANYWAY.

NO, I WON'T.

YOU WANNA TRY IT?

I KNOW MORE THAN YOU.

JUST WAIT AND SEE WHAT I DO.

YOU DON'T KNOW ANYTHING ANYWAY.

WANNA MAKE ME?

WHY ARE YOU DOING THIS TO ME?

YOU'RE JUST A STUPID BITCH/ASSHOLE.

SHUT UP.

FUCK OFF.

*(When you have finished reading the list, ask your responder/friend to open his or her eyes and turn to the next page.)*

What did you think of that little exercise? Revealing, wasn't it?

Inevitably, when I do this exercise as part of a training, the training participants answer the first couple of phrases in the following manner:

("You can't make me.") "Yes I can!"

("Leave me alone.") "Oh no I won't!"

("You're not the boss of me.") "Oh yes I am!"

("You don't know what I feel.") "Oh yes I do!"

Then the trainees start to laugh. They begin to see what is happening.

At this point, I ask them to keep responding to the rest of the statements on the list and watch what happens, what feelings and thoughts come up for them. By the time they get to the bottom of the list, the whole room is jabbering about what they felt and thought, and giggling with embarrassment about what they heard come out of their own mouths.

What did just happen? Well, as you probably already figured out, the list on the previous page is a set of typical statements adults report that children use with them when those children are picking a fight or when they are angry, defensive, wanting to blame, needing attention or testing rules.

In this simulation, as the adults listened to each of these goading statements by the 'child', and then responded spontaneously, time and again they reported they began to get flustered, or angry. Their breath quickened, their faces flushed, their hearts beat faster. They also reported they began to think negative thoughts about the child, thoughts about how to get back at "that kid"; or things they could say to make the child 'pay' for being disrespectful and abusive. They felt righteous, furious, justified. They even found themselves planning ways to continue to get back at the kid in the future. They imagined what they could do to the kid to punish him* for challenging their authority, for the rest of the day, week, (even months!).

Why does this happen so fast? What is it about a disrespectful, combative statement that sets us off so quickly? Why do we get hooked so easily? Basically, I think that it is human to defend ourselves against attack. We are quick to react to any hostility that comes from another person's tone, combative words, or physical stance.

The statements you just read/heard are hostile. To be sure, they are small assaults or mini-aggressions (except for the last one), yet, nevertheless, they are assaults. Each is an attempt to bait or blame us, put the problem in our lap, and make us think we are responsible for what the child feels. The child wants us to react with the same kind of statement with which he tried to bait us. And usually it works.

Power struggles are one of the hardest things to deal with when we work with rebellious kids. In my experience, nearly every time this topic is discussed among adults, the question arises, "Even though I am well aware of the uselessness of power struggles, why is it that inevitably I find myself embroiled in them over and over?" These adults go on to say something like, "Before I even realize it, I'm in the middle of one. And I am so frustrated with myself that I often make it worse. I get more and more stuck and defensive. Then I get angrier and angrier. I end up saying and doing things that I regret and my relationship with the child suffers."

When we least expect it, we clash with children over things that aren't very important, or in ways that don't further understanding and mutual respect. Even now, even after figuring out

*Although angry children come in both genders, to make reading easier, I will be using the male pronoun throughout this book.*

how to avoid many kinds of power struggles and successfully using the techniques I share in this book for many years, I still get caught.

Power struggles are probably the most difficult behavioral dynamic one can address with consistent and positive results. I am not sure why this is so. My colleagues and I wonder if it has to do with how vulnerable we really are as adults and in our roles as teachers, parents, caretakers--how much we really do give of ourselves, of our physical and emotional energy; how high our expectations are for ourselves and kids in our care; and how disheartened we feel when, over and over, we are disappointed by the children we love.

When kids deliberately start a fight, and our intentions were never anything but good, our first response is often hurt and anger. Our values, our legitimate power roles, and even our basic integrity are perceived to be at stake. Our emotions rise quickly.

But how do we stop before we react, or how do we extricate ourselves once we are hooked? How do we stop retorting in kind? How do we stop before we say something that gets us in deeper?

We have to figure out both how to short-circuit our natural responses so we don't create unnecessary struggles and how to do this when the child has already made his first combative statement.

Yet has the power struggle actually started once the child starts baiting us? Is the child's statement the actual point when the struggle begins? Does the child saying one of those negative things mean a power struggle is now inevitable?

These are common questions adults ask as they try to figure out what to do. For me, to each, the answer is a resounding "No!".

A power struggle has not started when a child attempts to goad you. The child's goading statement is just his verbally aggressive "plop". I repeat, <u>his</u>, not yours. Assuming your request of the child was fair and friendly, not punitive or baiting, you did not start/do anything. The child's statement is just one side of what could become a two-sided struggle. But it doesn't have to, because the struggle does not begin until...until what? Until you the adult respond in the same way, with the same kind of verbally aggressive statement!

Even if you take the bait by initially responding defensively, you don't have to keep responding that way. There are ways to either get out of the struggle or refuse to keep participating.

You cannot keep a child from initially wanting to win or gain the upper hand, but you can refuse to play the game. You don't have to respond in the same way. As long as you don't, there really isn't any struggle. The child's statement just sits out there, reverberating. Without a response, it is just one person's goading, venting or voicing of anger. It goes nowhere.

Further, it might help to remember that we adults do the same thing. We try to start power struggles just like children do. We can also avoid beginning one by not acting out our own anger or frustration on a child, by not baiting a child with statements like:

"Why are you being so difficult with me?"

"Get over here and get to work."

"You better do this now or else..."

"You're not in charge, I am."

"Just wait and see what I do, young man."

"Don't tell me what to do."

"You're beginning to make me angry, so watch it."

I have heard every one of these, and similar, statements come from the mouths of adults. Each of these is a defensive attempt to re-establish our power, a way to put the child back in his place. What they elicit is a "Try and make me!" response from the child. This is not a productive way to get our point across.

Power struggles don't just happen to us. They start when we start them, either with a goad of our own, or by negatively reacting to the goading of the child. Believe me, if adults who are in charge engage in a power struggles, the majority of children will fall right into the trap. Children get hooked easily too.

Further, power struggles are rarely about a particular problem, or what one has a right to say, do, or not say, not do. They are about deeper issues both for us as adults and for the children with whom we are clashing. That may be why they are so hard to extinguish as part of our repertoire of management mishaps. Given this, I think it is important that we become masters at addressing them productively.

This book is about creating a set of responsible responses to children's attempts to engage us in power struggles. That means both before we get embroiled in them and then once we have landed in the mess such struggles generate. In the process of reading this book and looking at the dynamics of such struggles with children, I hope you will begin to see ways in which you may unintentionally start these struggles too.

Remember: In a power struggle between an adult and a child, the only person ever responsible for starting that struggle is YOU, the adult. Given this perspective, in the following chapters I look at power struggles in depth: what they are, why they occur, why they often happen so easily, what we get from them, and how to deal with them once they have started. In the next chapter, I begin with my definition of the term "power struggle".

## Chapter Two

# *What Is The Definition Of A Power Struggle Used In This Book?*

The definition of a power struggle used in this book expresses the experiences my colleagues and I have had as we struggle not to fight with angry kids. Here it is:

**A power struggle is a push-pull conflict between two people, each of whom believes he or she knows more, sees more, can do more, and/or has the right to win (over the other). Power struggles are a clash of wills, a locking of horns. Each person is determined to force his or her position on the other through verbal (and some-times subtle, physical) coercion or intimidation. Neither party is open to incorporating the other's point of view, so the 'conversation' or exchange remains repetitive (it goes nowhere) and tends to spiral (escalate into higher levels of entrenchment by each party). Each person has an agenda based on being right. The message is: "I know the facts, the answer, the truth. I am right and you are wrong."**

Given this definition, in reality there need be no struggle. By role, the adult already has more power in the first place. However, that adult has forgotten this fact and, consequently, what has resulted is a personal, and inappropriate, role conflict between two 'equal' (yet really 'unequal') wills.

There are four assumptions that underlie this definition. *First, you, the adult, cannot keep a child from initially want-ing to engage in a power struggle, but you can refuse to take part.* By doing so, you end the option of a struggle.

*Second, as a 'locking of horns', power struggles are a special dance between two people that often takes each party by surprise.* The two parties clash in a surprising and primal way, like two fighting bucks, who, antlers locked, jockey and sway, as if drawn into a vortex.

Such struggles between an adult and child are often driven by two very different need systems at work, two sudden, often potentially explosive and opposing energies. The dance one observes is almost mesmerizing. It has a kind of wonderment to it. The clash is so intense, so direct, so locked into itself with the expression of counter emotions and righteous purposes, that it seems to have a life of its own that outsiders cannot penetrate.

*Third, when a power struggle occurs, the home, classroom or program environment is not a safe place to be — for any child.* Conflict between a child and adult creates an atmosphere of tension for all the people in that environment. In order to feel safe, the child wants to know that you the adult are in charge. But once you enter a power struggle, you no longer project the sense that you are in control of the situation. When a child doesn't feel safe, he focuses on the tension, not on the activity. As a result, he relates, attends, participates, or learns very little.

*Fourth, there is a natural and essential power difference between an adult and a child.* Oddly enough, power struggles are not an appropriate expression of that difference. Rather, they are a misuse and a misunderstanding of power by you the adult.

The struggle is about the adult's need to establish consensus, a reality that may or may not be achievable. It is about the adult trying to get control by forcing the child to honor (actually submit to) his or her authority, rather than simply asserting that authority regardless of whether or not the child agrees with that adult's inherent right to have that power.

You, the adult, have all the power you need to deal with a child's actions without getting into a battle to make your point. You have both role power and the ability either to defuse the situation, or to carry out certain consequences. However, to exercise that power when <u>in</u> a power struggle is counter productive.

By definition, there are no winners in a power struggle, because the purpose of each player is to vanquish the opponent through force of will, no matter who is right about the issue at hand. Given this, both players will ultimately lose.

## Chapter Three

# *What This Book Is And Is Not About*

*Try and Make Me! Power Struggles: A Book of Strategies for Adults Who Live and Work With Angry Kids,* is not about getting the right answers from the experts as to 'what to do from now on'. The strategies I will suggest in succeeding pages will not work every time with every child, nor are they the only ones you could use. I am certain there are other behavioral interventions you could implement that might work just as well.

What this book is about is sharing a number of interventions, discovered through much training, reading and practical experimentation, that have worked well for me and the many adults with whom I have lived and worked.

Further, this book's emphasis is on responding to a child's behaviors, as opposed to understanding the complex, underlying reasons why such behaviors occur*.

The emphasis is on looking at various kinds of baiting behaviors and then responding to them by picking effective preventive, avoidance and diffusion techniques. When confronted by a combative child, it is assumed that, in most cases, the adult has done much thinking about, as well as interacting with, the youth beforehand, so any intervention will be informed by this background knowledge and experience.

*\*In the best of circumstances, understanding the underlying causes is certainly important when developing a thorough picture of a human being's vulnerabilities, motives, and historical patterns that might contribute to any acting out. A thorough analysis should be part of every parent's process and an initial diagnostic protocol part of every professional's work. With such analysis, one is better "armed" when one enters a tough situation with a kid.*

Related to this, one of the fundamental premises I have when working with angry kids is that, regardless of the underlying issues, or the extent of one's history with a child, in the moment, combative behaviors need to be addressed no matter what. By definition, such behaviors detract from both the natural flow of interactions and daily routines. One ignores them at one's peril.

Regardless of either the quality of your relationship with a child, the child's past patterns, or specific internal or environmental influences, there will always be a behavior that requires an immediate response. The behavior is where the intervention must start. To respond well at this concrete level may impact both on the rest of that child's day and on many other levels of the child's reality.

*Of course, this multi-disciplinary perspective requires screening for many potential problems, which can create irritable, defensive, aggressive, negative, or impulsive kids, and then using the results of the screening to intervene. Children's problems can be primarily internal (within the youth's body and psyche) or external (environmental). More accurately, they might have developed due to a combination of factors. Such factors could include:*

1. *habituated responses which were adaptive to childhood life but maladaptive for older living,*
2. *psychological trauma due to childhood (or current) abuse, vision or hearing problems, visual or auditory processing problems,*
3. *other cognitive and motor weaknesses,*
4. *allergies, chemical sensitivities, glucose intolerance,*
5. *brain instabilities such as ADHD, ADD, bi-polar disorder, dyslexia, and*
6. *in a range of learning problems.*

*Further, many of the areas listed on the previous pages actually influence, promote and interact with each other so that it is difficult to determine what came first, or what is the primary problem at hand. For example, many professionals now know that certain brain traumas and chemical imbalances develop as a result of psychological and physical abuse. So the task of forming a unified picture is not easy, and, as such, would require a separate book to address properly.*

It is not necessary to have an in depth understanding of the dynamics or a kid's historical picture before intervening effectively. Realistically, it is virtually impossible to do this anyway when you are being confronted by the child in the moment. We don't usually have the time or training to assess visual problems, chemical imbalances, or a hidden abusive history, but we can at least act responsibly to address the observable, behavioral level. Getting past this initial interaction without increasing the conflict will give you the space to ask further questions and then plan for a less combative next-time exchange with the child. But not addressing the behavior purposively will increase the problem.

# Chapter Four

# *What Does A Power Struggle Look Like?*

Now, let's take a look at an example of what is probably a familiar kind of power struggle. This one is taken from a school setting, but a similar one could easily occur between a parent and child. It is a struggle between a 12-year-old student and one of his teachers. The student, Joey, is sitting at his desk, looking down at an assignment the teacher has just given to the class.

Joey: "I don't want to do this."

Teacher: "Why not, Joey?"

J: "Because I don't."

T: "But why not?"

J: "It's stupid."

T: "No, it's not. But why do you think so?"

(Silence)

T: "Joey, I asked 'why?'"

(Silence)

T: "Joey, you aren't saying why." (Teacher moves closer to Joey.)

J: "So...?"

(The teacher's eyes widen, her mouth opens...)

(Joey repeats…) "So what?"

T: "Ok, the 'so what?' is that I need to know why you are acting like this, to understand what's going on." (Teacher has hands on hips, her face has a frown.)

J: "Why? Who cares?"

T: "Because I want to figure out what's wrong. I want to help you."

J: "Sure. Okay. You can help me by me not having to do the stupid assignment in the first place! (Then mumbling in a lower tone of voice, Joey says,) I can't do it anyway."

T: "No, Joey, I can't let you do that. That's not an option. What did you say at the end there? I couldn't hear you."

J: (Joey mouths silently and with a sarcastic look on his face,) "That's not an option." (Then he shrugs his shoulders and says,) "I'm not gonna do it."

T: "Oh yes, Joey, yes you are."

J: "No, I'm not."

T: "Yes you are. You are going to do it whether you like it or not."

J: (Joey looks up at the teacher.) "You can't make me. Try and make me! You'll see what happens."

T: "Joey, if you don't do the assignment right now, there is going to be a big consequence."

J: "I don't care."

T: "Yes you do, you DO care."

J: "No, I don't. And don't tell me how I feel."

T: "That's not what I meant, Joey."

J: "Oh, yes it is. You think you know me and you don't." (Joey's voice is rising.)

T: "Well, in some ways I do know you. But I guess I'm learning other ways that I don't. I am surprised at your behavior, Joey."

J: (Joey stands up, fists clenched at his side.) "You don't know me. Leave me alone. You're stupid! This whole class is stupid!"

T: "You don't need to say that, Joey. The only one being stu…well, difficult now, is you."

J: "I'm NOT stupid. You are. You are the stupidest person of all! (Joey's face is flushed; his body is tense, hands clenched, his torso leaning forward as he speaks.)

T: (The teacher steps forward toward Joey.) "Joey! Stop right now! You have no right to speak to me like that. Nobody speaks to me that way."

(Joey starts walking toward the door.)

T: "Joey, stop.  Joey…!"

J: "I won't stop.  Too bad.  I'm leaving."
(Joey starts out the door.)

T: "Joey, Joey, please don't walk out. You'll only get into trouble. Stop, before it's too late!"

J: "I'm already in trouble.  I hate this class. I hate everyone in here."

(Another student pipes up,) "Go head, Joey. We don't like you either."

J: "Yeah.  See! "No one likes me!"
(Joey glares at the teacher.)

T: "Oh, come on, Joey. Yes they do.  Stop. You can still stop."

J: "No they don't.  I won't stop.  I'm leaving and never coming back.  I don't care anymore anyway."

(The teacher follows Joey out the door.  Joey heads down the hall.  The teacher follows calling down the hall for help. Another teacher sees what is happening and says, "I'll call for the Principal.")

Joey's teacher comes up behind him and puts her hand on his shoulder.  He jerks away and starts to run down the corridor.

T: "Joey stop!"

J: "Fuck you!"

(He runs around the corner out of sight.)

Yelps and sounds of struggling come from the next hall. The teacher rounds the corner, and there Joey is, being held in the gym teacher's arms, grunting and snorting.  His body slowly deflates and he begins to cry, "Let me go. Let me go."

The two teachers stand with Joey, talking with him for 10 minutes. Joey begins to calm down.  Joey and his classroom teacher walk over to the Principal's office to cool off, and then discuss what has just happened further.  A parent is called, Joey is put on suspension for a day, and then, still angry and hurt, he is sent home early.

Afterwards, the teacher returns to her classroom. There are sounds of laughter and shuffling as she approaches her room, students racing back to their seats as she enters the room. The floor is strewn with paper airplanes, the black board filled with doodles.  Exasperated, the teacher sits at her desk and frowns at the students.

"Class, please put away the assignment you were doing.  We will work on it later.  Get out your library books and read quietly to yourselves for a while."  (She closes her eyes and tries to figure out how to stop being so angry.  She tries to think how she could have avoided that struggle with Joey.  She ponders how to keep from having other struggles like this in the future.  She keeps asking herself, "Why did he get so upset over nothing? Why does Joey have to be so difficult? Why does he fight over everything? Why is his attitude so bad? I wasted all this time dealing with him, and, meanwhile, the rest of the class has deteriorated. I am not sure what to do to get things back on track." She puts her head in her hands. The students rummage around for their library books. The room is silent.)

\*\*\*\*\*\*\*\*\*\*\*\*\*\*\*\*\*\*\*\*

In the future, such struggles with Joey probably won't be avoided, because the teacher seems to have little idea the real reason why this one started. She has returned to class still caught in negative emotions. She thinks the fight is about Joey, his behaviors, and his difficult personality. Whereas, in truth, the struggle is really about her, the teacher.

This struggle between Joey and his teacher is the teacher's problem. She could have avoided it to begin with. His behaviors are just his behaviors. They will be there under the surface whether she fights with him or not. In fact, they will surely escalate if she does fight.

This example shows how easy it is to get locked in. It has all the elements of a typical 'tit for tat' conflict, the kind we all know so well. With each retort, the other person is jockeying for control and as each does so, the fight escalates, ending unhappily for both Joey and his teacher.

Further, as is also revealed by this example, as it escalates, the struggle begins to express other pertinent issues and themes held by each person. In this case, the teacher issue that emerged is taking Joey's "You're stupid" comment personally.

On the other side, Joey reveals one of his issues too. He fears he cannot do the assignment and that the other students don't like him. The struggle is a way for Joey to express those feelings without having to own up to them. He is probably trying to save face. The only way to do this is to struggle with the teacher. And being in a struggle is safer than exposing a learning weakness to peers.

So what could the teacher have done differently? When did the trouble really start? In this example, I think it started when the teacher, in answer to Joey saying: "I'm not going to do it (the assignment)", replies with "Oh yes, Joey, yes you are." By responding in that way; "tit for tat", the teacher has entered the battle. Instead of saying 'yes you will' to Joey's 'no I won't', the teacher could have done a number of other less confrontive things which might have enabled her to avoid a battle with Joey, <u>and</u> focus on the underlying problem earlier.

It might have been better to talk with Joey apart from the rest of the group, or set a limit and send him to the office at the first sign of defiance once she saw that her attempts at diffusion were ignored.

For example, the teacher could have said, "Ok, for now, don't worry about the assignment." Then she could have spoken with him in private about her expectations. Or she could have waited and not responded at all except with an inquiring face, and then observed what Joey did next. Then again, she could have given Joey some choices--suggesting he do the assignment with someone else, or do it differently. She could even have asked Joey to talk with her outside the classroom right then and there. That might not have solved the problem, but it would certainly have broken the whole-class tension and, with no one looking on, created the opportunity for a more honest, less combative dialogue between the two.

But it was clear that the teacher was getting exasperated by Joey. For her, getting the assignment done (by stating it was not an option not to do it) was more important than avoiding a struggle. I am not saying the teacher was aware of this at

33

the time. She was just reacting to each statement Joey made in the context of what she wanted him to do. She had forgotten that it could lead to an impasse.

How could she raise her own awareness while in the heat of the moment--as she begins to react to Joey's anger? What is it that let's us know we may be 'stepping into hot water'?

Let's say you are beginning to get irritated with a child. Let's say the child has done nothing purposively to annoy you or force a position on you… yet. But, for some reason you are annoyed with the child anyway. Maybe you are annoyed because the child is taking too long to finish something or do what you ask. Maybe the child is whispering things to other children, laughing in a disparaging way, making sarcastic remarks, ignoring your requests, making unnecessary noises, or failing to participate in an activity. Perhaps the child is refusing to do the work, like Joey. Whatever the irritating behavior may be, this is still prior to the child becoming directly goading. There is no struggle yet.

At this point, you still have a choice. You can still approach the child to try to discuss what he or she is doing; or if you choose, you can set a limit. However, if you decide to do something that baits the child, something that gives the sign that you want a fight, then you are starting a power struggle. The minute you say or do something that goads or baits the child (intentionally or not), you have started a power struggle.

Further, after a child has goaded or baited you, and you respond in a like manner, you are pushing for a power struggle. You know, all those little ways we all try to start a struggle, to "get back at" children in our care; to get them to behave when we are annoyed, or tired, rushed, and/or frustrated.

In these instances, we say to ourselves, "That kid just won't stop, will he? I'm gonna get him to be quiet if it's the last thing I do!" Then, in this state of mind, we approach the child and say something like, "Would you mind paying attention? I've asked you many times before. Don't you get it? You need to stop being difficult and listen to what I am saying."

Or we say, "I need you to stop getting all upset over nothing now and if you don't, things are going to get pretty unpleasant around here." Or we say, "Don't you have anything better to do than make noise? I am getting sick and tired of having to talk to you about this. Either do it or leave, please."

None of these statements seems very confrontive. You could see how an adult might say these things at one point or another to a child, especially when a child has a pattern of interrupting or disregarding instructions. But each statement is really baiting the child – to start a fight.

In the first set of statements, the "Would you mind paying attention?" is not a friendly, open comment, a first step to check out what is going on, what is wrong. Rather, the statement is slightly sarcastic and accusatory. With that kind of tone, such statements often have the immediate effect of making the child defensive.

Another troublesome sentence is "Don't you get it?" When we say that, we are implying the child is kind of stupid, and should know by now when to be quiet. (I imagine the child thinks in return: "Yeah, I get it, you idiot, it's you who doesn't get it! You're the stupid one!")

In another statement ("…things are going to get unpleasant around here"), the adult is threatening the child without being clear either about what the infraction is or what the penalty will be.

In the last few statements (like, "don't you have anything better to do" and "I am getting sick and tired…"), again the adult is being sarcastic as well as saying that the child is too much to deal with. Further, the problem of adult 'exhaustion' is addressed with only one solution, namely, the adult stays/wins and the child leaves/loses. In that scenario, there is no hope for reconciliation.

In none of the statements above, does the adult take responsibility for what he or she wants, with clear, descriptive "I" statements. And the child doesn't have a chance to speak to the issue before being sentenced. Chances are the child has done something disruptive, but it is often better to respond initially "as if" the child must have more of a story behind his or her actions than may appear on the surface. This assumption gives the child room to move, a reason to become engaged with you in a discussion rather than a battle. Even if the child's own first response is to explain his 'innocence' (however dishonest a response this may be), at least it is a starting point that enables you to move into the exchange rather than raise your ire against the coming tirade.

Young people need to save face in front of others, but often and especially when in front of an adult. They act like they want to stand out, look tough AND have the last word. Yet most of them are pretty thin-skinned. They do not expect an adult to really engage with them in return. In fact, they expect the opposite, and often begin eliciting negative reactions from adults on purpose, to bolster their view that relating to parents, teachers, or any adults, is 'for the birds' and that adults really are not interested in who they really are.

Here are some things you might say that are less combative:

> "Uh oh, what did I do to get you upset with me?"

> "Can we start over here? I did not mean for us to get into anything unhappy."

> "Boy, we have so many neat things to do today, can we talk about what just happened later? I need your help right now."

"If you are frustrated or upset, please take time for
yourself. It happens to all of us, and you deserve a
moment to stop and take stock. I'll leave you alone
for a bit."

"Is there anything I can do to make this day
go better for you?"

You can even just ask, "What's up?" (with a smile and
furrowed brow), and then back off and leave the child
alone. If you want compliance, the last thing you want to
do is return a child's goad with the same kind of response.
Yet, you should not ignore the action either. You can just
acknowledge it or set a limit, agree to talk with the child
later, and then return to what was going on before the
struggle started.

But regardless if you make the first move, or the child
does, you, the adult, are responsible for the fact that a
struggle ensues. I find that when I say this to adults they
acknowledge that they understand, but then I find that
they easily fall back into old patterns when they actually
are confronted with a real situation. This is true for me
too. As I said before, this is not an easy nut to crack. You
may know in your mind and heart that what you do makes
the difference, but acting on that in the moment can be
difficult.

However, don't despair! You just need time with the ideas
in this book, and opportunities to practice saying good
statements as well as trying out various solutions. My
colleagues and I find that doing these things increases
our ability to see the next power struggle coming.

The next chapter discusses the many common signs
we might encounter that warn us a power struggle might
be starting.

# Chapter Five

## *What Are The Signs A Power Struggle Might Be Starting?*

Over the years, the professionals, parents and children with whom I have worked, have identified a list of the typical signs that suggest a power struggle could occur. I think becoming highly aware of the many different things children (and you) can do to start power struggles, lessens the possibility of entering them. Some of the most common signs are listed below. See which ones are familiar to you.

The combative person:

– is arguing some useless point with you.

– keeps trying to get in the last word.

– says the same things over and over, and gets angrier or more agitated over time.

– keeps contradicting you.

– postures or has a combative stance, i.e. arms folded tightly across chest or hands on hips, chest and head are forward, fists clenched, face red, etc.

– makes dismissive gestures: makes a face, rolls eyes, slumps, turns away, etc.

– makes a sarcastic remark.

– keeps raising his voice.

– doesn't respond at all (as a way to prove a point, be right, win).

– is whining: "You're not being fair; you always pick on me."

– has a pinched face, narrowed eyes, and might be thinking: "Okay, this person is not going to treat me like this. I can last as long as he can. He does not know what he is talking about. Let's just see if he can make me do what he wants."

– is acting superior by puffing out his chest, raising nose, etc.

– is ordering you around, in an imperious, commanding tone.

– (with a blank face), is pretending neutrality on the outside while inside perseverating with vengeful thoughts about you.

– is standing with hands on hips, a snide expression on his face, cocked shoulders, while he may be thinking thoughts like: "Okay, he isn't listening to me on purpose; I'll just have to keep bothering him until he gets it." Or "I guess he'll have to learn it the hard way." "He's not going to get away with this." "We'll see who can make who do what."

"He's not going to get me; we'll see who's boss."
"I am stronger than him and I can make him do
what I want." "I'll make him pay; I can break him
down any time I want."

— when asked a question, is acting like he did not
  hear (but you know he did).

— is walking away when you are clearly speaking
  to him... then when confronted says,
  "Oh, I heard you, I was just going to do what you
  asked" (in a sing-songy, denying voice).

— is responding to a request with,
  "Oh, yes sir, I'll do it right away, sir",
  in an overly solicitous tone.

— is responding, but does not complete the task
  in a timely way... takes forever...
  or the task is completed without telling you
  and then when asked about it, says,
  "Oh, didn't you know, I did it already"
  (with an innocent tone or demeanor).

— is responding to a request with just a minimal
  answer, the least grunt possible.

Many of the signs on this list are subtle behaviors, what one
might call 'micro-aggressions'. They are the things we, the
responders, often initially 'second guess' ourselves about. In the
case of these small goads, for us as adults, we often sense that

the child is doing something weird, but then we deny our intuition. We worry we are overreacting or that we will just make it worse by assuming that the child has a negative motive.

It is also difficult to confront such behaviors, because they can so easily be denied. You might be accused of 'not getting it', overreacting, or just misunderstanding what the person reeeaaalllyyyy meant. The child will say, "Oh, you must have misunderstood me. I didn't mean that. I meant such and such instead." (And then he will try to start a struggle in the same way again the next day.)

But, believe me, if your intuition says something is amiss, listen to it.

It is true that there are some people who respond to every perceived slight with paranoia. If you think you are continuously overreacting to a child or, as a rule do not understand what is going on between you and that child, I suggest you get the opinion of a third party. Check out others' perceptions of the situation. Do they see the child the same way? Do they see you doing something wrong? Often talking with another adult who is not caught up in the situation, can help you differentiate between your issues and those of the child.

Further, each of us has a unique power struggle style. Different things trigger each of us, and we express our combativeness differently. Some of us are quieter, more passive aggressive, yet seemingly cheery and positive. We politely disagree, while underneath we are seething, making subtle faces when the other party is not looking, or muttering negative, critical comments when we walk away, or later to friends. Others of us become tense and rigid, or opinionated, picky and perfectionistic. Still others of us, assuming the worst, immediately overreact and attack our prey without mercy.

Each of these reactions is part of our own special style. Each of these defines the way we fight. Which one is most like you? And which ones characterize the way a child fights with you in return? The more we know both ourselves and the special ways children in our care "get their backs up", the easier it will be to divert and diffuse the first sign a struggle is starting.

In general, no matter the particular way in which the child or you begins a power struggle, the 'conversation' that ensues, (if you can call it that), has a number of distinctive characteristics. It usually has an argumentative tone, with you and the child talking at the same time, or talking over each other, with flushed faces and racing breath. Voices are rising. Everyone around you is getting quieter and either transfixed by what is happening, or trying to avoid the situation altogether. Other children might be chiming in, in the child's defense. You and the child are getting flustered, saying things you don't usually say and in ways you don't usually say them. You both are insisting on your own points of view. You are no longer listening before speaking over each other. You and the child are saying things that are building a case, making the situation bigger than it was in the beginning. What was once a small, initial defiance by one of you has turned into a 'global' fight.

Why, despite these signs do we still find ourselves embroiled in struggles over and over? The next chapter will focus on reasons why these struggles can be so enticing.

## Chapter Six

# *Why Is It So Easy For Us To Get Involved In Power Struggles?*

## *What Do We 'Get' From Being in These Struggles?*

It is very hard not to get caught up. We keep doing it even when, in the midst of a struggle, we can see ourselves getting in deeper and deeper. We all struggle to remain conscious and 'adult' when children bait us. But often we fail. A typical comment I often hear is:

"Penny, I did it again. The minute _____ (insert a child's name) said 'You can't make me do anything!', I came right back with, 'Oh yes I can!' Then I started arguing with him and twenty minutes later we were still going 'round and 'round. I could not think at all. I forgot everything I've learned. I couldn't even tell I was in a fight that was going nowhere until after I had heard myself repeating the same argument ten times. What is the matter with me? How come it's still so easy for me to get caught up like this? I know better."

There isn't any one reason that easily explains why we get triggered. Each of us is different. Each of us finds our combative child-self emerge at different times and in different ways. I think the best we can do is: each time we (finally) find ourselves outside the particular struggle we were just in and while we are still licking our wounds, we should try to identify the exact place where we got hooked. By doing that, often we can discover what makes us defensive. The more we do this the more we will be both aware of our triggers as they arise in the moment and prepared for similar incidents in the future.

*Why is It So Easy For Us To Get Involved in Power Struggles?*

Over the years, the adults with whom I have lived and worked have named many reasons they find themselves easily embroiled in power struggles with kids. Some of the most common ones are listed below.

*First, many people have told me that no matter how small the potential conflict, they think it is just an innate, natural tendency for them to defend themselves against an attack, an aggressive behavior, or even a 'micro aggression'.* They say it is often an automatic response. They cannot find any particular reason, they just find themselves reacting automatically to another's aggression, however distant from their own personal vulnerabilities.

*Second, many adults I know say they enter struggles because they need to feel like they are in charge.* Their sense of self esteem and prestige, their sense of self-importance, are based not just on feeling more powerful than someone else, but also regularly demonstrating that power. (This goes for the child too. The child may also feel he cannot afford to be vulnerable; that he only feels okay or safe when controlling others.)

*A third reason adults often give is that they think their past experiences might be triggering them somehow.* 'Getting triggered' means the present situation has some aspects that remind us of a past trauma. Often, not realizing it, we suddenly feel as if we are back experiencing some earlier, unresolved issue. We might even get triggered by a past situation that has little or nothing to do with what is going on now, but which is so powerful that it leaks into the present situation.

Often the feelings that accompany this reliving are very strong, stronger than the present situation warrants. For example, we could be triggered by a comment that another person makes, the tone of the comment reminding us of judgments our father used to make when we were a child. Or, we could be experiencing the present situation as similar to feelings of being abused by a former partner or parent.

Because the past experience is still an active, however repressed, part of our lives, we get thrown and start responding as if the earlier incident is actually occurring all over again. Because of all the strong feelings this elicits in us, we react without thinking, finding it difficult to understand what is happening to us in the moment.

*A fourth reason for our reactive stance is that we might feel affronted, our values questioned, and consequently, we are standing up for our position in the only way we know how.* For instance, if we have a strong belief that a child should finish what he starts, we might be unforgiving when the child refuses to finish something we have expected of him. We might have rigid beliefs or views of our role, like: "a child should always say 'Thank you'", "finish one thing before starting the next"; "be seen and not heard".

Or, our belief might be that the adult must always be the responsible one: "the adult must be responsible for teaching respect, cleanliness, responsibility, duty, etc., and must model those values consistently". In these cases, any defiance means a deeper value has been transgressed. We are fearful that any minor transgression signals that we are no longer in control of our values, so we respond forcefully.

*Another reason is that we might be entering a situation with an agenda, with a set view on something about which we want to preach.* We might have heard something about the other person, or be defending against an earlier encounter. We are not interested in finding places of consensus. Instead, we are interested in proving our position.

*Finally, we might have no good reason at all related to the incident itself.* We could be tired, burned out, in need of a break ourselves. We could have a gnawing backache or even have indigestion from too big a lunch. We could be thinking about an argument with our partner earlier in the day, and consequently find ourselves unable to focus positively on the issue at hand. After the fight, we might say, "I don't even know what I was fighting about. I wasn't even upset with this kid.  He does the same thing every day and it doesn't bother me, but for some reason, today it did. I guess I must be upset about something else and just taking it out on this kid."

There are many reasons for getting embroiled in a fight with someone. Most reasons are valid at some level. At some point, all of us act out our feelings. We are human.  However, we know it is better if we don't, especially when we are in a position of power and the other person is in our charge. Acting out on a person with less power is a triple whammy. It can induce fear, damage a relationship, and reinforce a value that power prevails!

*What do we get from being in power struggles?*

Power struggles are not always just negative events. There are often gains for both parties. The child 'gets' to blow off steam. The child gets peer status; he gets to posture in front of his peers. The child gets to stand up for himself, however inappropriately. The child gets ego gratification: "No one is going to push me around!" "I'm not a wimp."

Also, for children who know no other way to assert themselves, power struggles reinforce their belief that the biggest, baddest person gets the goodies in life. Children get to avoid doing things they do not want to do. Last, they get to avoid being vulnerable and avoid responsibility.

What are we, the adults, getting? We get many of the same things. We get to blow off steam. We get to feel our power.  We get to affirm certain values we hold without having to risk them being questioned by a "pipsqueak kid", as one adult told me. We get to avoid being vulnerable, having to relate, and having to take a risk with a child. We might even get to avoid the recognition that we can't really change anyone. Instead, we reinforce a common belief that we really can and should be able to control another human being, someone who is purposively bothering us, and by hook or by crook we are going to win!

Now that we have looked at ourselves, let us return to the children and examine more closely why they often want to start struggles with us.

## Chapter Seven

# *Why Do Children Enter Power Struggles in the First Place?*

Any kid anywhere can start a power struggle. These kids can be any age, in any setting. Kids who start power struggles are just being kids. They each have different ways of expressing frustration and anger, and of surviving. Some stomp their feet. Others manipulate quietly. Still others try to talk us to death. Joey, whom you met earlier, demonstrates the typical kinds of coping behaviors a youngster often displays when in a power struggle with an adult. He has a combative stance, he uses a frontal approach; and he is a determined to win at all costs.

Children have different reasons for provoking struggles. Here are six reasons why I think children start power struggles. Each tells us something different about the child, and in doing so, helps guide the strategies we pick.

The child may be trying to…

1) Cope internally: (Joey is an example of this kind of child.)

   *This child characteristically must manage intrusive negative feelings and moods. The child could be chronically irritated, physically tired, pervasively hurt by, or fearful of, something. The child could also be overwhelmed by the many demands being made by too many conflicting emotions. This child could be so frustrated that your most recent request has just put him over the edge. Or this kind of child is mood-driven and coping with some developmental problem or brain-based impulsivity that results in an unsettled internal state.*

2) Defend deeper values:

   *This child believes that you have offended him in some fundamental and important way. In the child's mind, you have disregarded his values or been disrespectful of his very being. So the child feels he must defend his personal integrity at all costs. Often this kind of defiance is based on social-develop-*

*mental issues with which a child is struggling. The child is trying a belief on for size, or trying to establish his separate identity as part of growing up. It might be that the child has decided that peer acceptance is more important than anything an adult can say or do to him. The child fails to differentiate between an important value he needs to uphold and an inappropriate behavior he needs to let go.*

3) Respond habitually:

*This child has learned over time to respond this way. He does not know any other way to respond. He has few words, little ability to identify feelings, or to separate anger from action. He has no alternative and acceptable behaviors in his reper-toire. Acting out is this child's only way he knows how to take care of himself. In the past this might have served him well at home or on the street, but it is a maladaptive response in the present situation. This child says to himself, "No one is going to push me around anymore." He knows the world is made up of the powerful and the powerless. There is no in between. So, he acts the only way he knows to protect himself and is then dis-mayed at, or stubbornly defensive over, the reaction.*

4) Get triggered:

*This child overreacts to something another person does. When someone affronts this child, however innocently, the child 'remembers' (usually unconsciously) some other similar hurt or past affront (that is unresolved) and gets defensive again now, even though this incident is not related, much smaller and different.*

5) Be 'top dog' to feel okay:

*This child only feels good about himself when he feels better than, stronger than, or smarter than the other person. The sole goal is to feel okay by feeling more powerful than someone else. When it comes to a skill or ability, the need is to be better at it than the other person. The person is not out to get the adult. He is just desperately trying to feel positive about himself. He may appear flip or indifferent, but when confronted, this child usually backs down, deflates, and shows some sign of remorse or embarrassment.*

6) Enjoy another's weakness:

> *Unlike #5, this child doesn't enter conflicts just to feel better or more powerful. This person also actively enjoys making the other person grovel. His purpose is to shame the opponent while feeling good about himself. This child does not feel much, if any, empathy. He has become deadened to another's reality. He only feels good when the other person is completely squashed and no longer exists in his mind as a fellow human being.*

In my experience #6 children are rare. We often mistake a #5 child for a #6, but rarely are #5 children really as mean as we think. The #6 child enjoys making the other person squirm. He won't back down no matter the consequence, and usually has a regular pattern of manipulation as well as intimidation (and possibly assault).

In my experience, the majority of children who start power struggles are doing so for reasons related to #'s 1, 2 and 3. They are just standing up for themselves. They are trying to manage what is either going on inside them or going on outside in the immediate environment. In the moment, they are doing the only thing they know how to do to defend themselves.

We tend to think these children's reasons are more sinister. Otherwise, why would they be defying us? We forget that one of the important developmental tasks kids face is exploring their own wills, their boundaries, their senses of self, and who they are and what they believe.

One way kids learn where they end and we begin is to take a stand and see what happens. That is what kids do. They try on ideas and tactics to see what works; to hear themselves think out loud; and to establish their identities. What better place to do that than through a power struggle where they can test the waters without becoming too vulnerable, or too exposed, and where often they can get immediate support from their peers.

Have you ever noticed that most kids who start power struggles start them when there is at least one other peer present?

Or when one other adult, whom they think might support them, is around? You won't find struggles happening much when you and the child are alone, or in the presence of a group of other adults. Rather, they happen when kids are less vulnerable and more visible to those who might side with them.

*Aren't kids just trying to get attention?*

One last point needs to be mentioned: When we talk about why kids try to start power struggles with us, we often say, "They just want attention". You will notice that none of the six reasons I listed included "Get attention". All acting out has an attention dimension to it. But just paying attention to a child, even in a proactive way, rarely eliminates the needs for power, control, affirmation of values, etc. Nor does it address deeper historical patterns or hurts that are being expressed.

While I would never say don't pay attention to any child who is asking for you to attend to him, I think the more important issues related to power struggles are those I have discussed. In some way, every child who goads us is trying to get our attention, but that tells me nothing about a particular child or WHY the child uses a power struggle to get that attention.

We too, the adults, try to get attention from children in our charge. We have the same reasons as the ones listed above. Because we want to be liked. Because we get triggered. Because we are tired or annoyed. To push a principle or value we have. To re-establish our authority. To feel okay about ourselves. Even to get back at a kid, or make the kid grovel. The only difference is that we have the power to stop those struggles before they start, or we can make matters worse by using our power to meet our own personal needs (or neediness), not the child's.

There are many ways to address power struggles productively. In the next chapter, I share those that, in my experience, have worked most effectively.

## Chapter Eight

# *What Are Some Effective Ways to Prevent, Avoid and Diffuse Power Struggles?*

Unlike violence and aggression, power struggles are more personal. They are easier to get a handle on. They are familiar areas of conflict children use to communicate with us, however ineffectually. Power struggles are 'micro-aggressions' with which we all can identify. Sometimes they are more subtle and harder to detect than outright aggression. They sneak up on us. But they are still ours. They are between us and someone we live with, know well, or have in a group or class we run.

By responding appropriately to individual struggles with our children, we are decreasing the likelihood that such struggles will escalate into larger fights. We may not feel we can impact on neighborhood feuds, harassment of the 'geeks' or outsiders by cliques of students in schools, gang wars, or "societal violence", but we can influence how those kinds of larger situations begin.

Here are some solutions that many adults with whom I have worked have used successfully to prevent, avoid and diffuse power struggles with individual kids. I have divided these solutions into three sets. Each set focuses on a different point in the power struggle process. The first, preventive strategies, are used before an actual struggle ensues. Hopefully, by employing one or more of these kinds of strategies, a power struggle can be circumvented altogether. The second kind, avoidance strategies, are helpful when we are just at the beginning of a struggle. They include ways to step aside when we are first being baited, rather than taking our own next reactive step. The third kind, diffusion strategies, are useful when we find ourselves already fully embroiled in a struggle and need ways to disengage.

## Preventive Strategies

Before a child actually says something combative, and before you, the adult, says or does something that provokes a struggle with that child, here are some preventive strategies you might try:

*1. Start each day anew, with no leftover emotional agendas with any child.*

You may still have things to discuss or consequences to implement from the previous day, but leave your resentment and anger 'at the door'. As part of this suggestion, throughout the day continuously check out your own emotional state. It is very important that you the adult maintain an attitude of neutrality, openness, ease and caring with the child. Once a consequence has been given, do not carry any leftover irritation or anger at the child into the next encounter, or next day.

*2. State your expectations up front.*

Before beginning any activity, state your expectations up front. Tell the child what you expect of him as he works, plays, competes, or participates in the activity with you and what he can expect from you. Your expectations would include what behaviors you want him to demonstrate or maintain and what you will do during the activity. Examples might be: "I expect you to take your turn, let me know when you have questions, and that you will put away your work/toys when you are done. I expect that you might have questions along the way. You might need a break while you work too. Things you can expect from me include me staying nearby to answer any questions you have, giving you a turn to speak, and listening to you without interruption."

Expectations can take many forms, and need not be a list of formal statements verbalized before every new activity. However, in general, no matter how you share what you expect, the message needs to be "I have thought this through ahead; I have certain beliefs about how I want things done, and how best to work/play together. I think that telling you, the child, ahead of time what those expectations are, creates an atmosphere of openness, fairness and trust. You know what you can count on. I respect your need to know what is happening to you before it happens; I respect your need to feel secure and supported as we work/play together."

### 3. Give the child choices.

I have found that, as with stating expectations up front, just giving choices to children can prevent grumbling and resistance. If possible, when a new activity or event is about to occur, give the child a couple of choices. This is particularly useful when you know the child might have some resistance to what you want him to do.

We all like to have some role in what we are asked to do. We all want to feel important, powerful, and able to make decisions about how we will do things. Each of us has individual needs and styles that are important to honor and incorporate as we move through our day. This is even more important for children who are just learning who they are, who are trying out different ways to do things, or who are testing out new personalities and skills.

Further, when offering choices, always make sure you can deliver the choices at that time! Don't offer choices that require lots of extra resources or special props, are not currently available, or just 'might be doable', but aren't yet.

Some kinds of choices that often work well for me include the following:

- Would you like to write in your journal about this event, or are you more comfortable speaking to someone about it?

- Would you rather paint or draw?

– Would you like to talk now, or wait until later when you have some more time to think about what happened?

– Would you prefer to work with another person/me or do this task alone?

– Would you like to join the group/family/class now or be left alone for a while, and then join the group/family/class later?

*4. Catch the child doing a good job.*

In a moment when you catch the child doing well at a task, praise him using very concrete words, which describe exactly what he is doing that you admire. You might say: "That drawing is beautiful. The way you drew the flowers makes them look like they are moving in a breeze." Or, "I loved how you spoke to your friend. You had a smile on your face, and you said exactly what you needed from him before you could play together again." Or, "When I was talking to your sister, I really appreciated it that you waited quietly, did not move around a lot, or make a face at her."

We tend to forget that even the simplest compliment is remembered, even the smallest gratitude is appreciated by each of us. Stating even obvious accomplishments, or saying "good job" each time one of our charges succeeds, creates a positive atmosphere for all, never mind increasing those all important brain peptides and endorphins.

*5. Honor the totality of the child's feelings.*

Children have many strong feelings, both positive and negative, when they are struggling with us. Often the most important thing we can do is just recognize and affirm those feelings.

We adults have feelings too. When I am driving home at night thinking about a power struggle incident, sometimes I let my feelings expand into a fantasy about winning a particular struggle with a child. It helps. It enables me to shunt off lots of anger and frustration, and, when I "let it all hang out" in the car, I get a certain sense of perverse pleasure that begins to dissipate the tension. This allows my negative, darker side to "vent" too. Oddly, in the midst of my anger and the images, I often realize how much I like the child.

In my role as a teacher, here are some of my "I won" fantasies. (Other teachers and parents who have heard about these fantasies say they have had similar ones themselves.) I have wished I could suspend the defiant student; lock him out of the school; or make him walk home in the rain (or preferably an ice storm). I have had fantasies of overstating the student's infraction to his parents in the hope that the child is grounded for weeks. I have imagined making the child wash the lunchroom floor and write, "You were right, Ms. Cuninggim, and I was wrong" 10,000 times on the blackboard. I've pictured out-yelling the child until he puts his hands over his ears and curls up in a ball in the corner squealing, "I'm sorry, teacher, I'm sorry". I have even imagined putting my hands around the kid's neck and shaking him until his face turns red.

Privately allowing these fantasies does not fuel my anger. Usually, I return to the real world more tolerant of the child and clearer about what really did happen between me and him. Fantasizing clarifies the situation by shunting off my negative energy and putting things into perspective. Fantasies enable me to begin to see the child's combativeness and my inability to respond in a positive way, as a challenge, a place for growth, not just a problem to be solved.

As a corollary, it is important to honor the child's strong feelings too. Here are some ways I do this: As a parent, when I make announcements that might create anxiety, I often purposively name that the child might be unhappy, scared, feeling anxious, or confused about the change. Or as a parent, I might speculate out loud about how I might feel if I were the child, then just move on to another topic without requiring a response.

In my role as teacher, I let children do all kinds of role-plays. With younger children, I construct one to one role-plays around issues of aggression, sometimes using popular TV and comic book rubber action figures. With older youth I set up role-plays as mock exercises to address a common social issue kids their age have. Role-plays encourage controlled expressions of anger, negative thoughts, worries, etc., as well as positive ways to deal with a troubling event or issue.

I might let kids describe both their strengths and weaknesses when it comes to a certain subject — making sure each has opportunity to share both, and that the positives outweigh the negatives. I talk about the personal habits and foibles of famous authors, or well known political figures who overcame obstacles, fought for justice, suffered yet succeeded. I tell stories that bring events to life. Sometimes I share my own weaknesses, angry thoughts, frustrations and fears.

I am sure you have many strategies as well. The point is, I try to remain aware of all sides, of the importance of giving expression to the full person, the whole situation, and that usually means not forgetting the negative side.

Our children will be facing their negative, fearful feelings throughout their lives. They will have to deal with difficult people and difficult problems again and again. The more these negative, darker sides are talked about, and the more such feelings are out in the open, the more children will accept them as they arise, and the easier it will be for these children to handle them.

*6. Maintain tight routines.*

To prevent power struggles, the building and maintaining of minute-to-minute routines is one of the most important tools you have in your behavior management 'tool box'. I think power struggles often begin to brew when children are left in unstructured situations, or when routines are changed too often or unwittingly. Signs might be a pronouncement by children that they are "bored", or "can't wait" for the next activity. They might say that they can't remember what they are supposed to do next because "things change so much around here". (Perhaps things do change... and change too much.) Or they might start fidgeting and wandering around when they have to either wait in line or wait for a turn too long. These times are often when peers start to pick on each other or on you.

When I've had a hard day at home or work, often the first thing I do is look at the day's routines. I do the same with my staff. At the end of the day when they come to me exhausted and cynical, or very angry at kids in their charge, I sometimes suggest that perhaps the routines were unwittingly altered or lax. I might ask, "Were there any changes in routine today that were unexpected? Did the kids complain at any point about something that happened that surprised them? Did you inadvertently forget to include a routine you normally keep to religiously? Their answers sometimes provide clues as to why the kids were difficult to manage, why a particular kid goaded a staff, why the staff were fighting with kids all day.

Often when kids don't feel safe, when events and expectations are unclear, left to chance, those kids act out. They test the waters to find the boundaries and what rules and routines they can rely on. Clearly stated routines leave little or nothing to chance. They provide a structure, a set of scheduled tasks that are known to all and that will be repeated reliably each day.

Like expectations stated up front, routines are something you can count on. Daily group activities and routines that happen regularly are designed to create safety, security, and a healthy community (because they are set up for all to carry out, and for the good of the whole group, family, classroom). Further, they promote positive group, family or classroom values.

Routines should never be set up or changed arbitrarily, nor should they be based on adult needs alone. When a routine is broken, the change should be stated to the child, and then the original routine reinstated as quickly as possible. Even free time, transition time, and individual, independent learning time should be formally scheduled. This scheduling should include sub-steps that are listed to fully explain and carry out the intention of the routine. Routines should be established that enhance the educational or home climate, bring different groups of children together at different times, and allow for the building of one-to-one relationships.

When children begin to disagree or argue with each other (or you), first look to see if a routine has been changed or ignored. Then, if there is a gap in time, a positive routine should be added to refocus the children in more productive ways.

7. *Set rules together with children and keep those rules to a minimum.*

When children and adults set rules together, everyone wins. Children have more of a stake in supporting what they create. Kids often perceive that we the adults are free and they are not. They think we can do as we want because we make money, have a home and a car and can make any decision we want.

They believe they have to follow the rules and we don't. They need to understand that everyone in a functioning society, home or classroom has to abide by certain rules, practices, principles, and laws, even adults. None of us is free to do what we want without any consequences. People who live that way usually end up in jail.

So why not have children take part in making the rules? That way they will have their views and preferences included.

That way there will be fewer struggles.

When creating a rules list, I believe it is best to state no more than 5-6 rules. Further, I always try to state them in observable and positive language. Don't do this, don't do that, often creates immediate resistance. I believe rules should be written around basic respect for each other and for property. I suggest rules be written like these some adults and children I know have created together:

- Brush your teeth well every day.

- Put your dirty clothes away.

- Thank the person who helps you.

- Respect others' property.

- Please wait your turn to speak.

- Be sure to put away your materials each time you finish an activity.

- Be helpful to others.

- Ask for help the right way.

- Throw out your own garbage.

- If you can't be nice, be quiet.

- If you are beginning to fight, ask for help.

Besides having a clear set of rules, it is important not to create any rules you cannot really enforce. Further, do not promise a consequence you cannot carry out. Each time you ignore a rule, each time you back down, you promote a lack of trust. The child begins to say, "Oh he (the adult) won't really do that; he never does what he says; I can probably get around him, because he often does not follow through."

In fact, when developing rules and related consequences, it is better to 'shoot low' rather than high. This means stating rules that you can control within your own limited classroom, program or family resources, rather than stating some grandiose, seemingly powerful and ominous rule or consequence you can never fulfill.

Last, a few words about keeping your list of rules and your consequences short. Don't use too many. Don't make your rules and consequences too complicated. Regarding rules, as I mentioned before, I would pick five or six that the child agrees will help keep order and promote respect. With regard to consequencing, keep the consequence simple, fair, directly related to the infraction, and something that can be carried out quickly. Then, once the child has done what he was supposed to do, don't talk about the problem anymore. Move on.

I have found that the longer the list of rules, and the more complicated the consequences, the more confusion there is, and the more you and the child have to return to the rule/consequence to remember what all the parts entailed. Children often tell me that the more complicated the adult demands, the more they think the adult THINKS they are going to act out, so the adult needs a whole bunch of rules or consequences to keep them in line.

### 8. Don't let your feelings dictate your response.

There are times when our own feeling or mood rather than the objective seriousness of a child's behaviors dictates the way (or whether) we confront or consequence a child. Sometimes it is just humanly impossible to avoid doing this. But, many power struggles could be avoided if we could differentiate our emotional state/needs from the child's actions.

If you get annoyed when a child doesn't do something the way you want him to, but his behavior doesn't cause a disruption, let it go. If you are unhappy with the way a child speaks to another adult, yet the child is still being minimally respectful and focused on the activity, don't correct the child or make an issue of his approach in order to "teach him an important lesson". If a child refuses to participate in an activity, it might not affect your ability to carry it out. The child's natural consequence (being alone) is probably consequence enough.

When a child begins to get off-task, don't always jump on him. Instead of confronting such behaviors, try to redirect the child with friendly eye contact, a smile, or by moving near the child. Then later try talking with the child to see if there is something else going on that is affecting his ability to take part.

### 9. Never nag, scold or use sarcasm.

I think nagging and scolding are two ways of behaving that we all know are inappropriate with children in our care. However, I think sarcasm is not a trait we necessarily see as inappropriate. We say, "Well, what's wrong with a little sarcasm. It lets the child know I am not happy with him, but, at the same time, it still keeps the exchange on a lighter level".

The truth is that sarcasm is not a light way to communicate. Sarcasm breeds defensiveness. Sarcasm is a way to avoid relating. Sarcasm is even sometimes a way to START a power struggle. Yet, we often use it anyway, because we often can get away with it.

For many years, using sarcasm was a part of my style of relating to children at my workplace, as well as at home with my own children. I thought I was being kind of cool or savvy to make a sarcastic remark. It also let them know I was 'in-the-know', sometimes better, smarter than they. Didn't most people laugh when I did it? Yes, and that made it all right to do. I thought it was a good way to get my point across without having to standup for my real views, or directly confront anyone. Using it was really about expressing my distaste with something, or protecting myself from uncomfortable interactions. It was a way to avoid responsibility for what I really felt and what I really wanted to say.

Sarcasm creates a distance between you and children. It creates tension, a sense that you the adult need to be given a wide berth, that you can't be fully trusted. Because, (the child's thinking goes), what if some day that sarcasm will be turned against me, the child?

Best to either say how you are feeling (frustrated, tired of fighting, etc.) or say nothing at all rather than speak with a sarcastic tone to a combative kid. All it does is cultivate a climate of defensiveness.

*10. Do not make any promises you cannot keep.*

I have found that there is nothing so annoying to children as adults who make promises they don't keep. If you want to get into a power struggle, a good way is to be inconsistent, to say one thing and do another, to promise all kinds of things you cannot follow through on. You may think the child will like you more, but, frankly, not keeping a promise creates distrust, resentment and anger. Often just one broken promise can fracture a relationship permanently.

Further, when you ask a child to promise you that he won't behave in a certain way again, you are in a losing battle. If the child's behavior disrupts your work or the activity flow, then be assured he has had a pattern of doing this kind of thing before and will probably attempt it again. Asking a child to change such a behavior "from now on" with one "I promise" is futile. It takes time to change, both for us and for the children in our care. Change happens over the long haul, once we feel safe and invested. There are no shortcuts.

*11. Exude enthusiasm while continuously challenging the child.*

One good way to focus a child's competitive spirit and excess energy productively is to say things like, "You aren't going to believe the next thing we are going to do!" Or, "I bet you've never seen something like this." Or, "I think you are the first person I have ever tried to teach/show this to in this way; do you think you can do it?" Or, to a group "For this next activity to work, you are going to have to work closely together. It might be hard to do, but I've seen how well you work in a team and know you can do it. I am so excited! Wait until your parents/friends hear about this neat thing you did!"

I have found that enthusiasm, joy, and positivism actually improve performance. They also increase the likelihood that a child will participate productively in an activity. Everyone likes to be around people who are fun, who are excited about what they are doing – even teens. Oh, teenagers might be standoffish at first, because being happy isn't cool, but I have found that such negativity rarely lasts very long if you just keep moving along with the activity, with a smile on your face.

12. *Focus on areas where you can find agreement.*

There are endless places where children and adults disagree, like around issues involving why children are bored, feel left out, mistreated, or misunderstood. Like why children say they should not have to go to school or why they tell us they come home after a party at night stoned, tired, ill, or spaced-out. You could argue with them about their rationales for days.

But regardless of these realities, you and the child both want to be respected and be heard. All children want to matter, to be 'seen', to be cared about unconditionally. Begin there, where you have common ground. Find something the child is saying or doing with which you can agree. You could look at how the situation makes the child feel or you could express how, given what happened, you might have acted in the same way too. Talk about how you had a similar experience in your life and how you handled it. Stay connected to the child's point of view until he begins to soften and is able to hear your side of things.

13.  *Talk less, use non-verbal cues.*

I think we all tend to talk a lot <u>at</u> kids. We want them to understand, to "get it", to have the benefit of our wisdom. We almost feel guilty if we have not said everything we know about a topic, regardless of whether or not the kid can even 'hear' us. We forget what it feels like to be on the receiving end of parental or adult preaching.

Do not talk too much. For children who think globally, are visual or kinesthetic learners, emotionally fragile, with short attention spans, language-processing problems, or who are fidgety by nature, too much adult talk can be very irritating. For adolescents who aren't interested in anyone else's point of view anyway, such preaching only alienates them further.

Instead of using your vocal cords, learn to use nonverbal cues to signal a requested change in child behavior. Such cues might include a raised eyebrow, a friendly frown, a soft questioning face, hands on hips, or a shrug of the shoulders. Each demonstrates as much as words would, without the grating tone preaching often conveys.

These are some of the preventive strategies my colleagues and I have used successfully over the years. I hope they give you some new ways to prevent struggles from even starting. But sometimes they start anyway. What follows are some avoidance strategies you might be able to use to help keep the tension from escalating into a full-blown power struggle.

## Early Intervention or Avoidance Strategies

Here are some good avoidance strategies to use on the brink of a conflict. These strategies will help when you are right at that moment when a child has first said or done something that could pull you into a power struggle, (but you haven't reacted yet).

### 1. Ignore the behavior.

Ignoring a child's baiting behavior is a tricky strategy to use well. In general, I do not believe that one should ignore any misbehavior. But sometimes when a child is trying to goad you into a fight, pretending you did not hear him, being 'busy' or preoccupied with 'other interesting things', or just not acknowledging his remark, might help you keep a struggle from ensuing. You might invite that child into your busy world at that moment hoping to refocus his attention.

Typically, I only use this strategy with children I know well, who can tolerate my ignoring their behaviors in the moment, or who know I will relate to them later about the problem.

### 2. Suggest wait time.

Slow down the tense exchange by suggesting that you each stop, "wait for a second", to highlight the fast pace of feelings and thoughts that are beginning to arise in both of you. Sometimes suggesting a "time out", even while still standing in the same place, stems the growing tide of combativeness. By doing this, you are not saying that what the child is doing is wrong or that his position is being negated or halted all together. Rather, you are just taking a breather, a time out, until you both can collect your thoughts.

This is particularly effective if you include yourself in this suggested 'wait time' scenario. You could say, "Hey, how about if we wait for a second here before we get into anything…I need some time to think about what I am saying." Or, "Oh, wait a minute, I can't keep up with this. I want to understand you. But I need a minute to get organized in my head. Is that okay?"

### 3. Give the child what he wants.

Sometimes you do not have to end up putting the kid back 'in his place', or righting the imbalance of power at all. Instead, you can give the child what he wants. Find some way to meet the child's request, even in part (provided you are not undermining your own purpose or needs).

For example, you could say: "Well, now that you are saying that, it seems to me that part of what you need is to take a break from what you are doing. Is that true? That is fine with me." Or, "Is part of why you are upset with me your fear you would not be included in the activity? If so, then let's see how we can include you."

*4. Redirect the child to another topic or activity.*

I call this the "hop over" strategy. What you literally do is hop right over the impending battle to some other topic of interest to the child by identifying something else somewhere else that is going on at the time of the child's potential conflict with you. Be sure to redirect the child with gusto, and never look back.

I might look at my watch and say, "Oh look at that, we are late to our next appointment. We need to get going. We can finish this later." Or, I might say, "Don't you want to do _____ before we get all mixed up in this fight? We can disagree about this later when we have more time to listen to each other's side, okay?" Maybe you say, "Oh, I forgot I was going to show you something you might like to do. Wanna see it now?" I use this kind of redirection strategy when I have a pretty good relationship with the child, he is easily distractible, or I know he is highly responsive to redirection.

*5. Stop, think, and ask questions about what might really be going on underneath.*

Try to figure out what is going on with the child as he begins to pick a fight with you. At this moment, I often find myself thinking, "This child really doesn't want power over me. What is the real reason the child is fighting with me now?" Then I run through the list of six reasons discussed earlier in this book. Is he trying to cope, defend a value, or build a peer base? Is he repeating a habit, getting 'triggered', trying to be on top, or just enjoying another's weakness? I try each reason on for size. I ask the child questions, which help me figure out why he or she got so upset. Then, when I figure out what might be going on, I focus on the reasons, not the struggle.

Sometimes this approach results in a clear answer which stops the struggle quickly. But even if it does not help to immediately end the conflict, this kind of reflective exercise helps me narrow the possible reasons and consciously choose my responses.

### 6. Set a limit.

Setting a limit is saying no, stating a consequence, and then if the child does not stop arguing or acting out, implementing that consequence. There are times when you need to confront a power play head on, as soon as a problem appears. This might occur when you have tried many things but a pattern of baiting still continues. It might be when you just don't have the energy anymore to go through another battle. Or you might just know the only way to stop the child is to say no firmly and then, if the child does not respond, give the consequence without discussion. Some children need limits without a lot of processing or explaining. Setting such a 'clean limit' sets a strong clear adult boundary.

When setting a limit you are using your power and authority directly. Who has the power is not negotiable. There is no debate. Your attitude is: "I am the adult and you are the child. This is the reality, period. And given that fact, I call the shots. I decide when enough is enough. I decide when to say no, and when to impose a consequence. Right now is the time."

When you set a limit, you are saying "no" and meaning it. "Meaning it" means you both can and will follow through on that limit. You do this by communicating a firmness and clarity when you speak; by giving the message that the consequence you name as part of that limit will be carried out if the child does not do what you require. You have the willingness and the ability, i.e., the emotional and family/program/staff resources to do so. You cannot and you won't be swayed. Do not set a limit unless you are able to follow through.

Do not say "no" or "stop" without knowing what you can and will do if that child does not listen to you -- if the child does not stop. Never set a consequence you cannot fully implement.

Setting a limit is a combination of common sense, attitude and follow through. Unless you have all three, I do not think you are setting a true limit. You might be confronting a child, grandstanding in some way, or displaying your role power, but you are not setting a limit that means anything. You are not creating clear boundaries. You are not building trust.

When you set a limit that is not based on common sense, but because "you said so", you have just created a power struggle. Someone is going to win, and someone is going to lose. If you win, you have undermined your role, your integrity; your sense of fair play. In effect, you become a bully no different from any child who might wish to bully you. Finally, if you lose (if the child "gets away with" something), you have undermined your effectiveness as the adult authority.

If you are not clear about your own control issues, then the child will pick up on this. This will create feelings of insecurity, anxiety, and alter the overall goal of whatever community the child and you are a part. An assumption here is that children want to know that we the adults are in charge. It is too much pressure (as well as being completely inappropriate) for children to believe that they are in charge, that they must take control of a situation in order to feel safe and good about themselves.

You are not in your role as adult to be in a personality contest with a child either. A child is not your "friend". You cannot keep secrets with him. You are not his "buddy". You can be friendly toward a child, you can share some of your own life experiences with him, but you are not on an equal footing.

If the child tries to join with you, cajole you, plead with you, badger you, or make subtle threats and you give in, your are undermining your own role as authority figure. You are also undermining your integrity, your ability to be firm and take a stand. When you do this, you are weakening your role as "commander and chief". The child will trust you less in the future. For each future incident, he will wonder what you are going to do, give in or stand up. Your boundaries are blurred, and, as a result, his own boundaries with you are blurred too.

On the other hand, if you can stay grounded in what you know and who you are; if you can maintain a reasonable sense of firmness, <u>and</u> remain focused on the issue, that is, on the behavior rather than the child, then you avoid the struggle and clarify roles. You are sending the message that you are in charge, that you are a safe, consistent adult who holds to your expectations of what is appropriate behavior when a child interacts with you.

*7. Step aside and provide choices.*

This strategy is really a martial arts principle. It means to get out of the way, create space or, as a martial arts practitioner would say, create MAI. You become a blank screen, serve as a reflective mirror, and let the person's own aggressive energy trip him up.

Anger and aggression are fire. If left alone they burn out quickly. Reactive statements are like adding dry kindling to a flame. They fuel the negative energy. When such negative energy comes at you, just step aside. Let the energy shudder in empty space, feed on itself. Let the child feel his energy reverberating, but with nowhere to go.

As part of stepping aside, you are giving the child space to make a choice. Explain the different choices that are available and the consequences of each. Allow the child to make a decision, accept that the child may make a bad choice, and then impose the consequence. This approach is neutral, respectful. It honors the child's independence, and that he really does control his own life and destiny. It keeps the debate on a higher plane. In this world, no one is free to do what one wants, when one wants, without consequences. This is not about who has the most power here. This is about deciding how to use one's power of choice.

It is important to remember that when you deliberately step aside and give the child a choice, you are not capitulating. You are engaging in a strategic move. You have made a purposeful decision to do this, so you still have control over the situation. You can choose to exercise this power at any moment you want; you don't have to prove you have it. Remember, you are the person with the family, school, or program rules behind you.

Also, try not to operate out of fear. If you are afraid that other adults will not support the consequence you want to impose, then rethink the consequence you set. Pick a more realistic one. Don't regress into a power struggle because you are stymied or out of frustration or defensiveness. Get the support you need or alter your strategy.

The 'bottom line' is that you should not be abused, scared, or intimidated by anyone. No parent can live that way with a child; no job is worth that.

However, let's say you try an avoidance strategy and it does not work. Now you are in the heat of battle. Below are some diffusion strategies you might try as a last resort.

## Mid/Late-Phase or Diffusion Strategies

Once you, the adult, find yourself deep in a power struggle, the best you can do is try to diffuse it. Here are some good diffusion strategies for climbing out of the stuck muck:

*1. Affirm the child's feelings.*

You can do this by showing that you are intently listening to, while reflecting on, what the child is saying. For this one to work, you need to stop being argumentative and demonstrate that you are listening carefully to the feeling tone of the child's words. You might move slightly closer to the child, eyes focused on him, with an open stance and nodding head. You might also say at some point, "I understand what you are saying. I can imagine feeling the same way."

But to say and do these things requires that you both feel empathy for the child and that you are able to step in his shoes in a moment when you might only feel annoyance. To genuinely affirm another's feelings when that person is affronting you is not easy. It takes skill and an ability to be open and somewhat vulnerable while both managing your negative feelings and remaining in control.

*2. Take responsibility for your part in the struggle and suggest you discuss your disagreement in private.*

By entering a struggle you are in fact embarrassing a child. As odd as that sounds, it is true. In some ways children have the right to confront adults. That is what children do. Then they have the 'right' to be consequenced. That is what we do in return, as part of our adult roles. It's an age-old game that is played out between adult and child. It is a game one can play fairly or unfairly.

If you enter the struggle, by definition the game is not fair. As the one in power, you are in effect trying to press the child into submission. Furthermore, you are likely doing this in a public venue! The child is now in an escalating struggle with a person who ultimately has more power. Further, it is likely to be going on in front of his peers or other adults.

No matter how much it seems as if a child wants to provoke you and win to boot, once it happens, another reality sets in. The child is now exposed for all to see. Bets are being taken. How is the child going to get out of this one? Will he be able to make the adult feel vulnerable? How will the child ultimately lose? Because one way or the other, lose he will, whether by being sent to his room, getting a "time out", being thrown out of class, losing weekend privileges, being suspended, or having to meet with the other parent, or a teacher, administrator, or counselor.

Instead, to avoid embarrassing a child, I think it is better for you to say something like this: "Hey, look, I'm getting into a competition with you. I'm sorry I am contributing to a fight between us. Why don't we talk about your concerns when I can pay full attention to you and when we aren't disturbing others. Can we talk in a few minutes? Can you do _____ or wait for a bit until I can sit with you?" These kinds of comments help the child both save face and quickly reestablish your relationship.

### 3. Respond with humor.

Sometimes it works to say something funny, not with sarcasm, but with a friendly tone, a statement or gesture that diffuses the tension by making everyone smile. You might say, "Uh oh, my heart is racing (breath, breath)...I am getting overly excited about all this. Oh dear. Help me calm down." Or, you could say in a dramatic tone, "Oh my goodness, I have to win this argument with you, I just have to or I won't be able to sleep tonight, will you? This is just the most terrible thing that has happened to me forever in a long time!" Or how about this one: (In a British accent) "I can't seem to get my point across 'ole chap. Perhaps I need a cup of tea; would you like to join me?" For each of these it is important that you are genuinely being playful, not feeling annoyed. What one feels underneath comes through no matter the words we use.

### 4. Create a forum for a power struggle simulation.

Another diffusion strategy is to engage in a role-play. This is not easy to accomplish in the moment, but it is often very effective.

If you can anticipate how the power struggle will continue to escalate, make the struggle into a role-play whose two parts you yourself simulate through a series of back and forth statements. Here is an example with me again in the role of teacher.

After I make a reasonable request of a stubborn child, he might say, "You can't make me do anything." In return, I might say, "Uh oh, guess what's happening here?" Then I go on to play out the dialogue by stating, "I could say, 'Oh yes I can', or 'You can't tell me that', and then you say, 'Whatever', or 'Try and make me', and then I say 'Then I will', and then you could say, 'Go ahead', and then, and then… what would I do then? Well, I would probably say 'Let's step outside and talk about this without disrupting the class', and you might say, 'No, I won't' and then I would say 'Why not? What is bothering you? Are you upset about your grade, or your weekend?', and you might say, 'It is none of your business', and then I would say 'But it is my business', and you might say 'Just go away', then I would say 'I have to call for the principal', or tell you, you have to leave class, and then you would refuse, and then I go get help.

Then I say, "Just look at what would happen: You go to detention and end up having to do work outside of here rather than being part of the class. All the progress you are making and good things you contribute are put 'on hold'. I bet I would get frustrated because I would wish I had never gotten into the battle with you in the first place. Neither of us is going to win anyway. Whew! Isn't this a mess? Is there some way we can go back to the beginning and do something different, so we don't go through all this and get into a long drawn out fight?" (Again, when using this strategy, be sure your tone is playful not mocking.)

*Here is another example:*

I say, "Uh oh, here we go! Me saying 'no' and you saying 'yes', then you saying 'yes' and me saying 'no'… and on and on. How about let's just put up our dukes and fight it out behind the barn?" (At this point, with a smile on my face, I would raise my fists-loosely formed, still below my waist — and sway a little in a silly, fun way.)

Sometimes what happens when I respond in one of these ways, is that the child actually interrupts my dialogue and corrects something I am saying. This could involve the child correcting what I suggest he might say or threaten to do, or the motives I attribute to the child. This interruption creates a crack in the child's own armor, and can be a gentle first step to understanding what is really going on and, consequently, suggests to the child how to respond in a less combative way. I have found that when I start acting out what might happen, the child begins to let his guard down, or sometimes the child stops, transfixed, and begins to listen carefully, even smile, as I present the made-up dialogue.

By no means will this suggested strategy work with all combative children. It usually requires that you and the child have had at least a few positive exchanges in the past, or even better, a connected, full relationship up to this point. If not, the next suggestion might make more sense.

*5. Stop pontificating, listen, set a limit, and give alternatives.*

Stop repeating your point; stop dwelling on the problem. You could just stop talking altogether. Endless adult chatter uses up too much energy and can escalate a conflict. Replace pontificating with a clear, simple limit and questions or suggestions for alternative, more positive behaviors. Here is an example:

"Whoops! I am going on and on, aren't I? I need to stop. (Pause.) I need to listen to you more carefully. You talk now and I'll listen."

Or,

"I'm saying too much. Actually, all I want to ask is, would you sit with me when I can really pay attention to what you are saying without distractions? Would you be willing?"

Or,

"Let me sit down. I need to stop and think about what you are saying." (Then, once you have heard what was said, respond favorably to the parts that you can support, and set a limit around those you can't. You could say something like:) "I understand and support such and such, but not this other part. You can't do that. The consequence for that is/would be _____. So let's think of a different way to get what you want."

Often just saying these kinds of things not only diffuses the argument, but also dissipates the whole struggle. The child feels like he will really be heard and contained. This occurs just by the fact that the adult stops in her tracks, briefly states her authority through setting a limit, and then reviews how she also might be contributing to the problem. The child gets two things — a sense that he is heard and that he is being heard within the context of the adult's role as responsible leader who will both take proper control of the situation and make sure it all ends on a better note.

### 6. Walk away from the tension (without leaving the battle).

In some cases, either when no other diffusion strategy will work or when you know walking away won't escalate the child, leaving often relieves the tension. This kind of walking away is not turning on your heel and marching off in anger or exasperation. Rather, this is more like backing off for a while. This strategy is as much an attitude as any specific action.

To "walk away", I have backed up a few steps and stood silently with a patient, calm look on my face; or turned sideways and moved away at an angle with either a pondering look or a "Yikes! Let me think a minute" expression on my face. On occasion, I have said, "Okay, okay, right now you win", and then I turn slowly and walk to another part of the room and sit down as if in relief. With any of these, the message is: For the moment, I withdraw my energy completely outside the circular dance between us. I capitulate for the moment. This is not a loss. It is a reprieve, a "time out" to regroup. No choices are given, no speeches are made. The struggle is then revisited later when the child is refocused and both you and the child are calmer.

\*\*\*\*\*\*\*\*\*\*\*\*\*\*\*\*\*\*\*\*\*\*\*\*\*\*\*\*\*\*\*\*\*

Each of the strategies listed above works well in some situations. How well each works depends in large measure on what the reasons are the child has tried to start a struggle in the first place. Given this, in the next chapter I suggest some good matches between reasons discussed in Chapter 7 and the strategies just shared.

## Chapter Nine

# *What Are The Best Matches Between The Suggested Strategies and The Reasons Why Kids Enter Power Struggles?*

Once you decide what reason or combination of reasons seem to be at the heart of a child's combativeness, you want to pick the best strategy or strategy options for that child's needs. I will lay out each reason for getting into power struggles, and then share strategies I think would work best for each reason. I will suggest strategies for each of the different points in a power struggle process: 1) before you, the adult, takes the bait (preventive); 2) just when you start to get caught up in a struggle (avoidance); and 3) when you are fully embroiled (diffusion).

### Reasons why children enter struggles:

*#1 Cope internally*

*#2 Defend deeper values*

*#3 Respond habitually*

*#4 Get triggered*

*#5 Be 'top dog'; to feel okay*

*#6 Enjoy another's weakness*

*#1 Cope internally:* If the child is overwhelmed by too many demands, or by many conflicting emotions; or if the child tends to be very mood driven, or impulsive, I would suggest the following strategies.

## Preventive Strategies

- *Honor and name the child's feelings.*
- *Give the child choices with a nurturing demeanor.*
- *Set clear and consistent rules and routines.*

All the preventive strategies listed in Chapter 8 would be useful, but I would be sure to focus on those particular ones named above that help the child slow down, and feel safe and protected emotionally.

## Early Intervention/Avoidance Strategies

- *Suggest wait time.*
- *Figure out what might be going on underneath and then honor that reality for the child.*
- *Step aside and provide choices.*

I would NOT ignore the behavior, or at the opposite extreme, give the child what he or she wants. I would also probably not redirect the child to another activity, because the child is too emotionally involved in what is going on now to be able to refocus easily. Last, I would probably avoid setting a limit unless it were a softly set limit, designed to gently redirect the child while he managed the strong feelings that had surfaced.

## Mid-Late Phase/Diffusion Strategies

- *Affirm the child's feelings.*
- *Stop pontificating, listen, set a (soft) limit, and give alternatives in a friendly way.*

At all costs, I would try to avoid contributing to an escalation of this child's emotions. Nothing can be accomplished between you and the child until the child is able to calm himself down first. Responding with humor or creating a forum for acting out a simulation of what is going on, might just exacerbate the emotions being expressed. Better to affirm and listen; then address the issues at a later point when the child (and you) are feeling less emotionally attached to a particular outcome.

*#2 Defend deeper values:* When a child feels like you have offended him in some fundamental way; if the child feels he

must define his personal integrity at all costs, then I suggest the following strategies:

## Preventive Strategies

- *Honor and support the values; differentiate values from behavior.*
- *Focus on where you can find agreement.*

Again, all the preventive strategies are useful here, but the two mentioned above are the ones I think best to use when relating to an angry child who feels affronted by something that you have done/said (even if you haven't!). They focus on affirming the child's feelings and strong sense that his integrity is at stake. They are designed to help find places where you can agree and honor the child's view, even if you do not see the situation the same way. Later you can talk about the way the child behaves and the process of the interaction.

## Avoidance Strategies

- *Name the values underlying the behavior.*
- *Set a limit (while supporting the child's feelings).*
- *Step aside and provide choices.*
- *Stop, think and ask questions about what really might be going on underneath.*

When nipping a potential power struggle in the bud, at least in part, I think one needs to address the child's bruised ego. It does not mean you cannot set a limit around the inappropriate behavior, but I would do that in the context of honoring that the child was emotionally affronted in some way, and that you are sorry if that has happened.

You want to remain as neutral as possible, as the child moves through his feelings of being disrespected. Once the child feels something has been "righted", a balance struck, you can then return to the activity or issue at hand, both of you intact. This kind of fight is not about participating or not participating. It is about an underlying sense of self that the child perceives has been hurt. Once the damage has been attended to, the struggle is over.

## Diffusion Strategies

- *Affirm the child's feelings.*
- *Take responsibility for your part in the struggle and suggest you discuss the issue in private.*
- *Stop pontificating, listen, set a (soft) limit, and give alternatives in a friendly way.*

As said above, the issue is the child's bruised identity, so the diffusion strategies designed to get you out of the fight should focus on easing back, on being conciliatory. Once the fight dissipates, and the child feels self-vindicated, there will be no struggle for justice.

*#3 Respond habitually:* When a child knows no other way to respond or keeps acting out a habitual or historical pattern, I would use one of these strategies:

## Preventive Strategies

All the preventive strategies I discussed in Chapter 8 work except probably "exude enthusiasm while challenging the child". Be enthusiastic for sure, but do not challenge this kind of child if he tends to get stuck unconsciously in old patterns of relating when stressed. Without being pushed too directly, this child needs to experience different ways of relating over much time in order to give up behaviors he is not even aware he has in the moment. Teaching alternative behaviors needs to occur when you and the child are in a neutral or more affable place. Of course, you can challenge him further in other skill areas where he already succeeds, while he is learning to relate differently.

## Avoidance Strategies

- *Suggest wait time.*
- *Redirect the child to another topic. Stop, think and ask questions about what might be going on underneath.*
- *Set a (soft) limit.*
- *Step aside and provide choices.*

Children who unconsciously act out old patterns need time and much attention to developing alternative acceptable behaviors to extinguish those patterns. A direct frontal limit does not make sense. I believe once the struggle is sidestepped, and you can represent your position as sensible and of friendly intent, the child might realize that what he is fighting about really is not that important to him now. With some careful coaching, you can show him that his response does not fit the situation logically, and may be related to some way he dealt with adults in his past or thinks you will respond, not how you actually have responded now.

## Diffusion Strategies

- *Stop pontificating and suggest alternatives that honor the child's position.*

I think the best diffusion strategy for a child with habitual patterns of defensive behavior is to stop arguing with the child and suggest alternative ways to deal with your differences. Other diffusion strategies like, taking responsibility, trying to respond with humor, or setting up a role-play simulation might just further entrench the child in his unconscious patterns. Best just to stop in your tracks and shift to a different way of handling the difference of views.

While in the heat of battle, you will not be able to convince the child that his reactions are old, inappropriate patterns that are no longer useful. That time will come later, in less heated teaching moments, and when he finds that the other new ways of relating he begins to both observe in others and experience himself, work better for him.

*#4 Get triggered:* When a child gets overly defensive in reaction to a perceived action of yours, an action which echoes in the same way as a past unresolved hurt, I would use the same sets of preventive, avoidance, and diffusion strategies lists for reason #1 above. Kids with reasons #1 and #4 need similar responses. The difference in the two relates to whether or not the strong feelings that come up for children come from their present cognitive or physical state OR come from a past, unresolved trauma. Both reactions need to be addressed sensitively and without a primary or direct confrontation of the surface behavior.

*#5 Be 'top dog' to feel okay.* When a child starts a struggle to feel good about himself; if he starts fights because he feels inadequate; if he acts up just to feel seen and important, then the following strategies might be the best ones to use:

**Preventive Strategies**

All the preventive strategies listed in Chapter Eight are important to use, but particularly:

- *Maintain routines.*
- *State expectations and rules up front.*
- *Be clear about whose problem this is.*

Kids with the 'top dog' syndrome need clarity of role boundaries. They need to know the rules and limits. They need clear expectations and responsibilities. And most importantly, they need consequences that are consistently followed through on. Using these strategies can often derail power struggles before they occur, because your demands and consequences are clear. These children need to be contained. Rules, routines and clear consequences are containing. At the same time, you do not want to create or enforce such rules and consequences rigidly. It is critical that you remain somewhat flexible around your expectations as you relate to these children. At the same time, because of their insecurities, these kids need much praise and many opportunities for success.

## Avoidance Strategies

- *Suggest wait time.*
- *Set a limit.*

For kids who try to win, who get into power struggles because they need a 'pride massage', the best avoidance strategy is a swift statement of "no." You do not want this kind of struggle to escalate. These kids respond best to firm, boundaried words and gestures. Suggesting wait time might work as a first step in the hope that the child will back down. But if this does not work, you need to quickly follow it with setting a limit. Period. No compromise. You can accompany the limit with some talk about what the child is doing that requires a limit, (i.e., his behavior demonstrates a self-involved attitude, a lack of caring and sensitivity); or you can offer the child another chance later, in a subsequent interaction, but the demand needs to be clear and focused on the behavior now, as he is attempting to start a fight with you.

## Diffusion Strategies

- *Respond with humor.*
- *Create a forum for a power struggle simulation.*
- *Stop pontificating, listen, set a limit (with clear, simple consequences for failure to comply), and give alternatives.*
- *Walk away without giving up the battle.*

For top dog kids, I think humor sometimes works. Without any sarcasm, but with a playful tone, I sometimes mimic what a kid is saying, mirroring back his statements. Sometimes this alone gets the child to see how ridiculous his position is - how it does not take anything into account but what HE wants, what HE should have, or how everyone else should meet HIS needs regardless of what is happening.

I also find it helps to speak outside the situation as if on stage. Kids with overblown egos often enjoy watching you role-play them. This is a kind of mirroring as well, but with more drama and more serious intent.

Of course, walking away for a minute or stopping your own arguing and setting a limit is the best fallback position. As mentioned earlier in the avoidance strategies section, top dog kids need limits. They respond to clear consequences. They may not like it. They might protest more strongly in return. You may want them to "understand" why you are setting consequences by explaining why, but frankly, these kids really don't need or appreciate your explanations in the moment. They want a line drawn between their behaviors and your tolerance level. Frankly, they are much more capable of working on their issues when not in the heat of a battle, when they are feeling good about something they have accomplished.

*#6 Enjoy another's weakness:* For kids who want others to grovel, use these strategies:

## Preventive Strategies

- *Use all the preventive strategies, but be sure to focus most on setting and consistently enforcing the rules.*

## Avoidance and Diffusion Strategies

- *Set a limit (with clear consequences).*

For children with the conscious desire to hurt someone else, who have little or no expressed empathy, I think this is the only avoidance or diffusion response that makes sense. It is better to avoid such struggles this way as soon as they start to emerge. But it requires much awareness of your own triggers. It requires that you not click into that natural "fight or flight" response one has when first attacked. It requires a fast shift into setting a neutral but unflinching limit. Once you are embroiled in a struggle with this kind of kid, you need to stop yourself from arguing as quickly as possible.

I suppose you could listen to the tirade from the child for a minute or so, then immediately acknowledge you "hear" him but that he needs to stop now, and if he doesn't you say what will happen next. If he complies with this request, the struggle is over and you are back in charge. But if he still does not respond, I would then institute the consequence immediately.

**********************************

The strategies discussed above are just some of the matches you could make for the various reasons children attempt struggles. Of course, this assumes you can figure out in the moment what a child's potential fight patterns are or what the reasons are for his goading behaviors. Sometimes you can't know, or you can be wrong. You could pick the wrong reason, only discovering that AFTER the strategy you use fails.

My general rule for working with combative kids is to institute, and carefully maintain, all the preventive strategies I have listed. Then with kids who start to bait me, I try to remain quiet, sitting inside myself, watching and listening until I figure out what the child needs, and what to do. I try not to take the bait, by making even one first combative gesture or comment in return. I talk with the child separately as much as possible, and I focus on building relationships with each child each day we are together.

Of course, I still find myself hooked sometimes. When I do, I return to the avoidance and diffusion strategies I talked about in Chapter 8. It is interesting that over time, I find that figuring out the children and the right strategy for each situation get to be second nature. I also find that as I improve my ability to build meaningful relationships with children in my care, the fewer struggles they start. Oops! Not "…the fewer struggles THEY start", right? What I meant to say is "… the fewer struggles I start!"

## Chapter Ten

# *What Should Replace Power Struggles? What Kinds of Relationships Should We Have With Children In Our Care?*

Power struggles are filled with raw energy, the first require-ment for developing a close relationship. Struggles are places where we can begin to relate differently to troubled kids, who, given their family histories, school failure, puni-tive management, and social isolation, have rarely taken risks to relate in positive ways. For many children, power strug-gles are a first strange step toward intimacy. But to access that connection, we, the adults, can't get caught.

Building relationships is an art. We adults assume we know how to relate to children in healthy ways. But often we don't. We think that if we have successful adult relationships those must transfer to kids. But the two are not the same. I have never seen an adult education course focused on relating appropriately to children, on building quality relationships as a way to enhance a learning or living environment and pro-mote feelings of self-esteem. Yet much research tells us that having a good relationship with one's adult mentor is one of the most important contributors to both a child's self-confi-dence and his/her success in life.

Further, more often than not, there were few good role models for us. Most of our childhood, familial, religious and school mentors were pretty straight-laced, formal, removed, and stern. For instance, in school our teachers usually stood in the front of the room and talked endlessly at us. Our homework was answering the questions in the back of each chapter of our text-books. We sat in rows, quietly and attentively, and only raised our hands when we were asked a question. We all did the same things at the same time and usually in the same ways.

We became highly adept at maneuvering through the world of adult authority. School was teacher-centered.

However, some of us were lucky. We had a positive mentor, someone who was able to both push us to do better, and nurture us in the process. It might have been a favorite uncle or grandparent. A caring teacher or choir leader. In whatever role the person played, he or she gave us unconditional regard.

A relationship of this type is a great gift to a child. In many instances, such a relationship can have a long-term impact on our life and career choices.

I would like to end this book with such an experience from my own childhood. It was with a teacher from my fourth grade elementary school in Dallas, Texas, almost 50 years ago.

Unlike this fourth grade teacher, my first grade teacher had over 40 children in the class to whom she related like a cowgirl corralling a herd. One half colored with crayons while the other half took turns jump-roping and swiveling with two hula-hoops on the playground. I don't remember my first grade teacher ever speaking individually to me.

My second grade teacher was rarely present in class. When she was out, she left me to read Oz books to the rest of the students and let us out to go to the bathroom without a chaperone, even when we didn't need to "go". I did like being "toilet monitor" though. (I was in charge of flushing when the rest of the children were done.)

My third and sixth grade teachers wore girdles, heels and frowns most of the day every day. My fifth grade teacher had all that and more. She washed my peer students' mouths out with soap, screamed at us, and was overly interested in our peer relationships when she matched us boy-girl, boy-girl for the many classroom games, gym exercises and dance performances she oversaw.

The only friendly, genuinely warm (yet also firm, 'no nonsense') adult I had in elementary school was my fourth grade teacher, Mrs. Bynum. I adored her. Mrs. Bynum was short, stocky, warm and solid. She was also very clear about her role, what was important, and what she expected from her students. I think she loved to teach. I knew she cared about every student the same, and she took the time to get to know each of us, demanding excellence and accepting the inevitable conflicts a large group of students in a class can produce.

My mom said I used to come home every day announcing, Mrs. Bynum says this or Mrs. Bynum says that. She was why I entered the field of teaching. What she gave me was a close adult relationship. She was interested in my stories. She read my assignments carefully, commenting on every idea. She spent time with me, and with every child, learning what we liked and did not like, what we did well and what came harder to us.

Recently I found a report card from her class. Before I opened it, I thought she must have given me all S+'s, but when I looked, it was not so. I found some S's and one S- for talking too much (but she did include a positive comment about how much I had improved). At first I was taken aback that I would like an adult so much who gave me some less-than-perfect marks, but then I realized she was probably right about me. She knew me well. She made me feel good about myself while, at the same time, being honest about my problems and pushing me to excel.

What I wanted and got from Mrs. Bynum, and what I know all of us wanted as children, were relationships with our adult mentors based on our unique interests and needs. Someone with a gentle touch, who never resorted to a power struggle to get us to behave.

What we want as adults is for children to interact with us in respectful ways that allow us to mentor them. But with children in our charge, we rarely are able to fully establish a relationship before they begin to annoy us.

To get the kind of respect we want, we need to do more than set our own expectations. We need to learn about the children in our care. We need to find out what they like; how they play and learn best; what their family circumstances are. We need to be interested in their lives, their dreams, not just in what they can accomplish in our classrooms, give to our activities, or contribute as part of our families. We need to be able to just listen, to share our own similar experiences, and look for the many (often conflicting) feelings that underlie almost every interaction they have with us. We need to both set firm limits and remain genuinely connected, even when affronted by a child on one of his bad days.

It should be remembered, though, that even if you have a good relationship with a child, you might still get embroiled in a power struggle. In fact, some children act out even more intensely around adults with whom they feel safe. What is important is that you value the building of a relationship with each child in your care and use that relationship to handle positively the first signs that a struggle is brewing.

Just trying one positive strategy can increase the chance that a struggle is short-circuited. Remember, you have the power. Use it to help kids make better choices. This is the best, the only way, to win.

## Appendix

# *Adult Training Worksheets*

On the following pages you will find some worksheets you can use to explore the ideas about power struggles discussed in this book. These worksheets are intended to both elicit your own personal experiences with power struggles and provide you with practice using the ideas in this book. Adults I work with say these exercises help embed the ideas more deeply, especially when they can work with them using their own unique experiences and ways of approaching their work with kids. Adults also like these exercises because they can use them to work independently and at their own pace as they learn and integrate new responses into their intervention repertoires.

# WHAT DO YOU THINK?

This exercise can be used to become more aware of how we think about power struggles. Finish each sentence with the first thought that comes to mind.

A power struggle is…

When I am in a power struggle I usually…

The kind of person I get into power struggles with the most with is…

The worst power struggle I ever experienced was….

If I saw two children in a power struggle, I would…

A power struggle really has not started until….

The worst thing about a power struggle is…

I think kids get in power struggles with adults because…

The only good thing about a power struggle is…

One can avoid power struggles if…

When in a power struggle with their child, parents should…

# PICKING YOUR OWN AVOIDANCE STRATEGIES

On the left, list out some common baiting behaviors you normally deal with. Then come up with an avoidance strategy for each that you think might work to keep you from getting sucked into a struggle that a child is signaling he or she wants to start with you.

| *Behaviors (Words or Gestures)* | *Avoidance Strategy* |
| --- | --- |
| | |

# PICK A RESPONSE

For each combative statement below, write a response that helps avoid or diffuse the situation. The first one is done for you.

| *Combative Statement* | *Good Response* |
|---|---|
| SO WHAT! | 'So what'? The 'what' is that I care about you. |
| YOU CAN'T MAKE ME. | |
| LEAVE ME ALONE. | |
| YOU'RE NOT THE BOSS OF ME. | |
| NO ONE IS GONNA LISTEN TO YOU. | |
| YOU DON'T KNOW WHAT I FEEL. | |
| NO, I WON'T. | |
| YOU WANNA JUST TRY IT? | |
| I KNOW MORE THAN YOU. | |
| JUST WAIT AND SEE WHAT I DO. | |
| YOU DON'T KNOW ANYTHING ANYWAY. | |
| YOU CAN'T TELL ME WHAT TO DO. | |
| YOU'RE SO STUPID. | |

# MAKE A PREVENTION PLAN

Review the suggested power struggle prevention strategies listed in the book. Then write out your own prevention plan below. Be sure your plan fits your own circumstances as well as your teaching and intervention styles, strengths and interests. Use the set of strategies suggested in this book as a guide. You may think of other strategies not included in this book. You may decide to have very few to start with. Begin with what you know will work.

| *Preventive Strategy* | *How/Why This Strategy Will Help Me* |
|---|---|
| | |

# PICK ANOTHER RESPONSE

Let us say that you ask a child to do something reasonable. You are not baiting him, nor are you annoyed or frustrated. The child does not say anything, but makes a gesture in the passive aggressive, disrespectful, or combative ways listed below on the left. For each combative gesture below, write a response that helps avoid or diffuse the situation. The first one is done for you.

| *Combative Gesture ~ The Child...* | *Good Response* |
|---|---|
| Walks away. | Catch up to the child and make friendly remarks. |
| Puts head on desk. | |
| Starts talking to someone else. | |
| Makes a negative face at you. (Rolls eyes, has a sarcastic smirk, etc.) | |
| Gets up and goes to another part of the room and starts doing something else. | |
| Shrugs and stands there without saying anything, eyes on the floor. | |
| Tries to stare you down. | |
| Gestures rudely. | |
| Points a finger at you and makes a menacing face, i.e. slit eyes, scrunched mouth, etc. | |

# STRUGGLE STARTERS

Here are some names for types of kids who start power struggles. Giving each type a name has helped me recognize what type I am dealing with in the moment, and consequently, I can often come up with the appropriate response more quickly. Please do not think that I am minimizing these kids' problems by using these titles. Doing this has helped me focus on the right response and keep a sense of humor.

See if you can figure out which ones represent which of the 6 reasons why students start struggles: that is to cope, because of habit, to seek justice, because triggered, to be top dog, or to make one grovel. *(Answer Key on next page.)*

| | |
|---|---|
| *Know It All Nora* | *Lonely Lucy* |
| *Contrary Carla* | *Impulsive Ira* |
| *Offended Olivia* | *Premeditated Peter* |
| *Tired and Grumpy Grace* | *Out of Control Oliver* |
| *Frightened Freddie* | *Overwhelmed Oscar* |
| *Pathological Patrick* | *Self Protective Susie* |
| *Triggered Tootsie* | *Insecure Iona* |
| *Righteous Rona* | *Hungry Hanna* |
| *Innocent Iggy* | *Homesick Hortense* |
| *Take a Stand Teddy* | *Vicious Victor* |
| *Peer-driven Patty* | *Puffed-up Parker* |

# Answer Key for the Struggle Starters Worksheet:

#1 Cope internally

#2 Defend deeper values

#3 Respond habitually

#4 Get triggered

#5 Be 'top dog' to feel okay

#6 Enjoy another's weakness

---

*Know It All Nora 5*

*Contrary Carla 3, 4*

*Offended Olivia 2*

*Tired and Grumpy Grace 1*

*Frightened Freddie 1, 4*

*Pathological Patrick 6*

*Triggered Tootsie 4*

*Righteous Rona 2, 5*

*Innocent Iggy 2, 3*

*Take a Stand Teddy 2*

*Peer-driven Patty 2*

*Lonely Lucy 1, 4*

*Impulsive Ira 3*

*Premeditated Peter 6*

*Out of Control Oliver 1, 3, 4, 5*

*Overwhelmed Oscar 1, 4*

*Self Protective Susie 3*

*Insecure Iona 1, 2*

*Hungry Hanna 1, 3, 4*

*Homesick Hortense 1, 3, 4*

*Vicious Victor 6*

*Puffed up Parker 1, 2, 3, 5, and 6*

## Picture Your Struggle

Draw a power struggle you were once in with a child. In the first frame, show how it started, in the second frame, draw how it looked at its peak. In the third frame, draw how it ended.

How are each of these scenes different? What happened as you moved through the struggle? What insights do you have about how you like to struggle with this child and how you get out of power struggles with him/her? What insights do you have about this child? Others? What would you write as a caption for each drawing? What does that say about you? To make things turn out differently, how would you change the drawing(s)?

# IF YOU INSIST

If you insist on winning, here are some great things you can say (on the left). After you read the list and have a good laugh, try to change each statement to a sentence that diffuses the struggle.

I GOT HIM, DIDN'T I?

TOO BAD, SUCKER!

MAKE ME.

I CAN MAKE YOU DO ANYTHING I WANT.

YOU WANNA TRY IT?

GET OUT AND DON'T COME  BACK!

I'VE GOT YOUR NUMBER, KID.

OH YES I CAN TELL YOU WHAT TO DO.

I AM THE BOSS AND YOU BETTER KNOW IT.

JUST TRY IT, KID.

# WHAT'S THE STORY?

Remember a struggle you had with a child. Tell the story to a friend or colleague without judging what you did. Just tell the story.

Now ask your friend to repeat the story back to you.

What new things did you learn about yourself from listening to the story as told by the other person?

How did the story change as it got told by each of you?

Does the story in either version embellish the truth? Does either avoid some part of the situation? Does the way the story was told, reveal what the teller got from being in the struggle? How do we alter stories to protect ourselves?

Each of you say one good thing about the situation — something you learned from (speaking or hearing) about it.

Is there some way the situation helped the adult or the child? What might be done differently and better next time? How might any of the ideas in this book help either of you reflect on this situation differently now?

# WHICH STRATEGIES DO I USE THE MOST?

Make a list below of some of the strategies you now use successfully to deal with conflicts with children in your charge. Then, put a P next to those that you believe are Preventive Strategies; an A next to those that could be considered Avoidance Strategies; and a D next to those that you think are Diffusion Strategies. Now ask yourself, what kinds do you use the most and which ones overlap? What does your list tell you about your preferred ways to deal with struggles, and what does it tell you about changes you might need to make?

Key:  P  = Preventive

A = Avoidance

D = Diffusion

*List:*                                *Type of Strategy:*

# NEARI PRESS
70 North Summer Street • Holyoke, MA 01040

## *NEARI PRESS TITLES*

*Enhancing Empathy* by Robert E. Longo and Laren Bays (1999).
Paperback, 77 pages. $12.00 plus shipping and handling.
Bulk discounts available.
ISBN#1-929657-04-8

*Growing Beyond* by Susan L. Robinson (2002). Paperback, 216 pages.
$20.00 plus shipping and handling. Bulk discounts available.
ISBN# 1-929657-17-X

*Growing Beyond Treatment Manual* by Susan L. Robinson (2002).
Paperback, 42 pages. $15.00 plus shipping and handling.
Bulk discounts available.
ISBN# 1-929657-15-3

*Men & Anger: Understanding and Managing Your Anger* by Murray Cullen
and Robert E. Longo (1999). Paperback, 125 pages. $15.00 plus shipping
and handling. Bulk discounts available.
ISBN#1-929657-12-9

*Moving Beyond* by Thomas F. Leversee, LCSW (2002). Paperback, 88
pages. $20.00 plus shipping and handling. Bulk discounts available.
ISBN# 1-929657-16-1

*Moving Beyond Student Manual* by Thomas F. Leversee, LCSW (2002).
Paperback, 52 pages. $10.00 plus shipping and handling.
Bulk discounts available.
ISBN# 1-929657-18-8

*New Hope For Youth: Experiential Exercises for Children & Adolescents*
by Robert E. Longo with Deborah P. Longo (2003). Paperback, 142 pages.
$35.00 plus shipping and handling.
ISBN# 1-929657-20-X

*Paths To Wellness* by Robert E. Longo (2001). Paperback, 144 pages.
$20.00 plus shipping and handling. Bulk discounts available.
ISBN#1-929657-19-6

*Respecting Residential Work With Children* by James R. Harris (2003).
Hardcover, 163 pages. $35.00 plus shipping and handling.
Bulk discounts available.
ISBN# 1-929657-21-8

*Standards of Care for Youth in Sex Offense Specific Residential Treatment* by S. Bengis, A. Brown, R. Longo, B. Matsuda, J. Ross, K. Singer, and J. Thomas (1997, 1998, 1999). Paperback, 71 pages. $40.00 plus shipping and handling. Bulk discounts available.
ISBN# 1-929657-05-6

*The Safe Workbook for Youth* by John McCarthy and Kathy MacDonald (2001). Paperback, 210 pages $20.00 plus shipping and handling. Bulk discounts available.
ISBN# 1-929657-14-5

*Try and Make Me! Power Struggles: A Book of Strategies for Adults Who Live and Work with Angry Kids* by Penny Cuninggim (2004) Paperback, 112 pages. $15.00 plus shipping and handling. Bulk discounts available.
ISBN# 1-929657-23-4

*Using Conscience as a Guide: Enhancing Sex Offender Treatment* in the Moral Domain by Niki Delson (2003). Paperback, 104 pages. $25.00 plus shipping and handling. Bulk discounts available.
ISBN# 1-929657-22-6

*Using Conscience as a Guide: Student Manual* by Niki Delson (2003). Paperback, 52 pages. $10.00 plus shipping and handling.
Bulk discounts available.
ISBN# 1-929657-19-6

*Who Am I and Why Am I In Treatment* by Robert E. Longo with Laren Bays (2000). Paperback, 85 pages. $12.00 plus shipping and handling. Bulk discounts available.
ISBN#1-929657-01-3

*Why Did I Do It Again & How Can I Stop?* by Robert E. Longo with Laren Bays (1999). Paperback, 192 pages. $20.00 plus shipping and handling. Bulk discounts available.
ISBN#1-929657-11-0

***To order call Whitman Distribution 800.353.3730***
Shipping and Handling $4.50 for one book.
$.50 for each additional book
Find us on the Web at: www.roblongo.com/npress.html

# Notes

# Notes

# Notes

# Notes